The Smoking Horse

THE Smoking Horse

A MEMOIR IN PIECES

Stephen Spotte

State University of New York Press
Albany, New York

Published by State University of New York Press, Albany

© 2010 State University of New York

All rights reserved

Printed in the United States of America

No part of this book may be used or reproduced in any manner whatsoever without written permission. No part of this book may be stored in a retrieval system or transmitted in any form or by any means including electronic, electrostatic, magnetic tape, mechanical, photocopying, recording, or otherwise without the prior permission in writing of the publisher.

Excelsior Editions is an imprint of State University of New York Press

For information, contact State University of New York Press, Albany, NY
www.sunypress.edu

Production by Kelli Williams
Marketing by Fran Keneston

Library of Congress Cataloging-in-Publication Data

Spotte, Stephen
  The smoking horse : a memoir in pieces / Stephen Spotte.
    p. cm. — (Excelsior editions)
  ISBN 978-1-4384-3139-0 (hardcover : alk. paper) 1. Spotte, Stephen 2. Marine biologists—United States—Biography. I. Title.
QH91.3.S66 2010
578.77'092—dc22
[B]
                                    2009026795

10 9 8 7 6 5 4 3 2 1

Everything that happens once can never happen again. But everything that happens twice will surely happen a third time.

—Paulo Coelho, *The Alchemist*

For Cap and Uncle Dirty,
who were there

1

*T*he same spring I got kicked out of boarding school Larry turned seventeen and said he was joining the Air Force to fly jets. Plus his mama had just given birth again and the only place left for him to sleep was on the floor. It seemed his mama was forever nursing a baby in the one stuffed chair while his daddy, who always looked tired, leaned against the doorjamb wearing workpants and an undershirt and smoking a cigarette, his suspenders hanging loose, probably because he had nowhere to sit.

Now that Larry's daddy had literally fucked him out of a bed Larry wanted Bob and me to join up too, but Bob couldn't because of Sharon. He said he needed to stick around. Larry told him that Sharon was an ugly bitch and mean besides; I said I was thinking about college. College? they hooted. You can't even get through eleventh grade.

Larry quit school and joined up without us, a four-year hitch. He got a bed of his own, although the closest he ever came to jets was hosing the dust off them. Not long after boot camp they stationed him in the Midwest where he met some other enlistees from West Virginia. All had come of age lacking a gene for depth perception, the evolutionary result of generations born and raised against the short vistas of mountainsides.

The bunch of them went drinking one afternoon, none fit even sober to sight down a straight road backed by a full horizon. They were heavily among corn, was Larry's memory, weaving close to the stalks and passing a bottle, when they came to an intersection doing about eighty and clipped a truck carrying pigs. It had seemed so far away, that truck did, visible from the top of a gradual rise and moving across them at ninety degrees. Larry was riding shotgun. At the moment of impact the windshield briefly interrupted his face as it passed through followed by the rest of him. The Air Force sent him home for good looking like a chewed steak and dragging along a sorry limp that never went away.

That was 1959. I was back from school in Maryland and living with my parents and baby sister Jane in a coal camp called Mallory in the southwestern part of the state. It was twenty miles from Kentucky as measured in a straight line. Daddy was plenty pissed at me but working too hard to think much about it. He was a mining engineer and superintendent at the mine. The company he worked for owned all the houses, for which the miners and their families paid rent. There was one store in the camp, and the company owned it too. If you worked at the mine you could buy groceries and clothes and even appliances there on credit, a form of indentured servitude because the more you bought the more got subtracted from your paycheck, and there was still that rent to pay. Nobody ever got clear.

Because of Daddy's job we lived in one of the better houses. I think there were seven of them. The rent was twenty-five dollars a month. These were dirty white structures with rolling porches clustered on some of the camp's little bit of bottom land. They were situated off to one side of the company store in two rows of three and then ours, the outermost, squashed beside the train tracks and the Mallory Road and not far from the entrance to Nigger Holler where the coloreds lived. Mr. and Mrs. Susong's house was catercorner to ours. Mr. Susong had charge of the company store and made sure everybody's credit was straight. He wore the thickest glasses anyone ever saw. Mrs. Susong was bony and a chain-smoker with the voice of a frantic elf trapped in a barrel. She was friendly in a coughing way and eventually died of emphysema.

Mr. Crawford was general manager of the mine. He was fat and smoked cigars through his bushy moustache and always looked surprised, like a shocked walrus. He and his wife lived in a big white house a little higher up the mountain. The Mallory Road ran the length of the camp along our side of Huff Creek, and on the other side was the hard road. Just past our house the Mallory Road curved up and over the train tracks where it split in two. One part continued to Nigger Holler and the other became the Crawford's driveway. Unlike ours, their house received fresh white paint now and then, and those high walls reflecting under sunlight gave off that pinkish glow you see on a Greek postcard. The company owned it too.

The rest of the houses, unpainted shacks in severe decline, stretched out along the opposite side of the company store, extending partway up the mountain. They were connected by dirt roads that washed away every spring and then people had to park by the store and walk home. When the ground dried out Mr. Crawford sent over heavy equipment from the mine to fill in the ruts.

The coal camps were unincorporated, and Mr. Crawford was a sort of unofficial mayor of Mallory. There were no police, but people mostly minded their own business. The lack of a fire department was more serious than the average domestic dispute. The company houses, heated by coal stoves, were dry tinder waiting to burn, and fires were common in winter. Then any men off shift who were drinking and loitering on the steps of the store would rush to the storeroom to get out the big pump with lots of hose and drag it to the creek. After being sure the suction end of the hose was submerged, someone removed the trap cover and started priming the pump with buckets of water while someone else labored to start the gasoline engine. This usually took some time, and meanwhile others started uncoiling the discharge hose and straightening it out so it could be pulled closer to the fire.

While all this was going on the rest of us—the men and boys—formed bucket brigades and started a chain that stretched from the creek to the stricken house, but if it was too far gone the water was thrown on adjacent houses to keep them from catching fire. Sometimes we broke our backs for hours, failing in the end to save much of anything.

Trains carrying coal from the tipples went past our house so close I could almost reach out my bedroom window and shake hands with the engineers. A passing train caused the whole house to shake and the china cabinet to rattle, and then conversation stopped because nobody could hear anything else. The trains crept slowly past, cars filled to capacity, wobbling and lurching and creaking, whistles blowing every few feet to warn children picking up spilled coal to take home and drunks lying across the tracks.

The train tracks generally had more pedestrians than the Mallory Road. One reason for this was a spring that dribbled out of the mountain close to where the road to Nigger Holler crossed the tracks. The spring was the camp's main source of water for drinking and cooking. Well water in that area was high in sulfur. It had a rotten egg smell and if used for cooking left a ring of dirty yellow crystals in the pan.

Parents sent their kids to the spring for water almost every day, and there was always a parade of them tripping along between the ties with jugs hanging off their fingers. You saw black kids at the spring too, all of us waiting in line to fill our jugs. Once there you had to get up to the source if you wanted clean water because right beside the spring was a pig pen. Occasionally a pig got loose and wallowed in the spring until someone chased it out.

I often saw El or Ed walking the train tracks carrying a sack and picking up coal, a gray image stumbling in and out of the mist. I can't recall their last names, but they were identical twins, mentally retarded, with El being the worse off. They must have been about fifty and lived by themselves in a tiny shack beside the tracks just outside the camp, surviving mostly by collecting bottles along the hard road and turning them in for a penny each at the company store. El was also supposed to deliver newspapers to subscribers in the camp, but there were only a few and he generally forgot where they lived. For this job he had an old red bicycle with a basket on the front. Ed did simple jobs such as raking leaves for people who could afford it. There was little routine to their days, or so it appeared to me, and they had no family around. Although their lives seemed outwardly like random turns into narrow corners, in our lack of pity it was the rest of us who were incomplete.

El couldn't take any teasing. The littler kids liked to walk up to him and shout, Hey El, crazy man! Ol' Republican! El's face would turn red as he chased after them, lumbering along surprisingly fast, the kids screaming in real fear until he suddenly forgot what he was doing and stopped. Then his face regained its normal appearance, which was squinty and pained and turned up slightly as if seeking out birds in flight. The kids would come back quietly to touch him and pull on his fingers, to look up at his empty eyes and wonder at his strangeness. El ignored them completely, not sensing their presence, his mind twisting through fractured memories.

Near the back edge of the open field behind our house was a large hickory. Sometimes we heard odd sounds and through the pantry window could see El with his arms wrapped around its trunk, pressing his face into the shaggy bark and yelling something sad and incoherent about the darkness. On days of no wind, when everything was silent, El's voice carried like a tortured soul's begging release from the eternal fires. He often stood there hours at a time shouting at no one until Ed found him, pried his fingers loose, and took him home. Then El was like a frightened child, and Ed talked gently to him, saying, It's okay, I got you boy, let go now, we're going home.

Huff Creek, an affluent of the Guyandotte River, was wide, shallow, and black with coal dust from the tipples. Occasionally when the tipples shut down the water would clarify and then only the rocks were black. Hardly anything survived, although I walked over and checked regularly hoping to see a fish or maybe a crawfish. On certain mornings mist dropped over the creek like a dustbin's worth of dirty glass shards emptied out against the light, and then the whole world turned monochrome.

Even in the best times you noticed convoys of turds from the outhouses upstream and toilet paper veils pinned to branches trailing over; half-inflated rubbers bobbed like life jackets in search of victims; cans and bottles, old tires, broken dolls, anything unwanted or undigested might appear one day and be gone the next. People mostly called it Shit Creek. If you asked another kid along the bottom where he lived he was likely to say, Up Shit Creek.

Spring rains were an annual cathartic. Rainwater sluicing off the mountains funneled into the creek turning it swift and brown. Everything that had stuck to the sides was swept away downstream leaving other objects in their place when the level subsided. Each year the view was different but still like a Picasso painting, one where he glued bits of junk to a canvas and stirred around the background.

Nobody ever swam in that water, although people were dunked there on occasion. Mallory had a small church of an uncertain denomination. Its preacher was a coal miner, tall and thin. He was darkly bearded with stringy hair and the dazed beatific expression of a Christ painted on black velvet. During special Sundays the congregation trudged along the tracks from the church, scrambled down off the railroad bed, and walked across the open field to the creek. There the preacher, resplendent and looking holy in a white robe, immersed his flock one by one in the black water, breaking through ice if necessary, and blessed them among the shit and flotsam, promising eternal life. Sometimes the worshippers passed El clinging to the hickory tree, but the preacher never turned his way even when El shouted, But the darkness! It's always the darkness! Perhaps El's demons were too potent, too vile and mysterious, to be driven out by mere baptism and prayer.

The train tracks passed through many of the coal camps along the bottom, but the hard road connected all of them, and that was how the older kids got to school. For junior high and high school you took a bus to Man several miles away. In front of the company store was a short one-lane bridge across Huff Creek, and at the end of it off to the left stood a three-sided structure with a roof where Mallory kids waited to be picked up. During the years I was in eighth and ninth grade an older kid who went to the high school waited there too. He said he was twenty, that he'd quit school to work in the mines but that now he had quit the mines to attend school. He collected wood and wind-blown paper and made fires on cold mornings, and he gave us cigarettes because we couldn't afford to buy our own. He was lacking some frontal teeth and wore a cap with a pointy brim.

On warm mornings the boys sat on the concrete railing dangling their feet over the side and spitting tobacco juice. Sometimes we threatened to throw someone into the water, but we never did. Just the threat was enough to keep the girls huddled in the bus stop, where they stayed even on sunny days.

From Mallory the bus went through a mostly empty area called Long Bottom where Larry Redman lived. Larry and Bob Phillips were my best friends. Larry was small with a pinched face and slits for eyes and looked vaguely feral, like one of his ancestors had shared carnal notions with a fox. His house was maybe five rooms not counting the outhouse, and he lived there with his parents and six siblings. Larry was the oldest, and his brothers and sisters all looked like him. They were smudged and tattered and abnormally watchful, as if plotting escape to a wide clean place.

The scenery around Larry's house and elsewhere along the bottoms gave an appearance of rampant vegetable mange, rutted and hardscrabbled and hopeless as a crippled orphan. Everywhere a blocked-up Hudson or Chevy minus its wheels oxidized beside a peeling house the color of decay. Here and there someone kept a lean cow or some pigs, and in summer you saw staked tomatoes and maybe a patch of corn stuck to a hillside or squeezed into the corner of a sodden yard. Any featured lawn was likely to be stained by a patchwork quilt of multi-colored cats. It all spoke of ignorant resignation, of invisible shackles here in the Land of the Free.

Coming into Man from Long Bottom you encountered Buffalo Creek, a larger festering version of the stream that flowed past our house. Along its banks were exoskeletons of ruined cars and trucks with their headlamps staring out, the crinkled grills vaguely mandibular and predatory. Surrounding them lay tires and leaking batteries and sacks of garbage, rotting upholstery and rusting engines, sprung seats where people once fucked or a drunk miner punched his wife in the face: offerings of sustenance for the mechanical afterlife now marinating in coal dust and acid water.

Sometimes the organic participated. One cold Saturday when a teenage girl was babysitting Jane, the two of them drove into Man. They pulled over upon seeing a crowd gathered at the creek. A dead man frozen in the dirty ice was staring skyward like a detail from a hillbilly still life rendered in black and gray. Taking the scene to be real the girls panicked and bolted from there in fear.

Bob lived in Man with his mama and little brother. Bob was lanky with a hunching posture, bad complexion, and a smile that crinkled his face about the eyes and forehead so you never knew if he was ready to laugh or cry. His older brother Ronald J. was around occasionally when he wasn't off in the military or in jail. There was no daddy in sight. Larry and I never asked questions. We figured his daddy was either dead or had run away.

Bob at least had a grandfather, which was more than Jane and I could claim. Our maternal grandpa had died of pneumonia when Mama was a junior in high school, and Daddy's father had been killed when the roof of a coal mine fell on him. He was an immigrant from Italy, and Daddy, like Mama, had been a junior when the accident occurred. Mama's father was a kind man, but Daddy once told me our paternal grandpa had been a mean bastard. He'd been fired as a mule driver in the Italian Alps for beating his mules, and that's when he decided to come to America and become a miner. Just one photograph of him exists, a sepia portrait of a grim square-jawed man with steely eyes and handlebar moustache.

Man was an actual town. It had a bar called the Smokehouse Grill, schools, and streets with names on them. There was a gas station and probably some stores, although I can't remember what they were. Across from the junior high was a fry shack where the kids gathered before morning classes and at lunchtime. Girls played the jukebox and danced with one another while laboring on gum and looking up at the ceiling, pretending they didn't know boys were watching. They shaved their legs and wore bobby sox and tight sweaters. It was a time of great confusion and encroaching lust. You could buy a plate of fries, a bottle of Coke, and a slice of bread and butter for a quarter. The fries came served on a real diner plate along with a metal fork, and just as you sat down half the population of Man Junior High came over asking for just one little fry and maybe a piece of your Coke.

When deer season opened in autumn lots of boys skipped school, and so did a few teachers. Deer season was a big event. Men who hunted spent lots of time rearranging their shifts so they were off during daylight. Those who didn't hunt and agreed to switch shifts with someone else were in good positions to bargain for cases of beer and cuts of the carcass if the hunt was successful. Larry's daddy didn't hunt deer and neither did mine, and Bob's daddy was nowhere around, but you saw lots of men wearing hunting outfits and kids whose parents could afford it wearing them too. Nothing looked dumber than a little kid stumbling along wearing an orange vest and hunting boots.

Anyone who shot a deer paraded it through Man tied atop his vehicle. There was lots of waving to friends and honking the horn. Shooting a deer was a hillbilly rite of passage similar to circumcision in certain other cultures, but also a form of heroism, and a guy with a ten-point buck on his hood was treated like the general of a liberating army.

On especially nice Saturdays the denizens of the Smokehouse might drag chairs outside to watch the parade, pulling on their beers and hawking lungers on the sidewalk.

Holy damn! one might say. That sumbitch has got size to it. Looks like a clean heart shot, I do believe.

That ol' Doggie's pickup carrying it? What kind of weaponry might he favor?

He got him a thirty aught-six last I knew, but that don't appear to be no heart shot. I've kilt many a deer and I'd recognize a heart shot.

You damn liar, you ain't never shot nothing bigger than a squirrel.

And just how would you know?

'Cause we'd be hearing about it every day of our goddamn life, that's how.

Sometimes Bob thumbed to Larry's house or mine and asked us to help him reason with Ronald J., who was nasty and always beating the hell out of someone. After quitting school he was in the drunk tank so often that a judge gave him the choice, either live there permanently or be a patriot and serve your country. Ronald J. joined the Marines, then was promptly discharged for fighting. After more jail time he somehow got into Army Special Forces and managed to stick. Once when thumbing home on leave a carload of Marines jumped him on the hard road just outside Man. Ronald J. beat them so badly they needed medical treatment.

But sober he was a different person, telling people he was truly sorry and shaking their hands all around, even people he didn't know. You'd see Ronald J. standing on the sidewalk smiling like a deranged evangelist, pumping the hands of patrons as they staggered out of the Smokehouse confused and light-struck.

Yep, hidey, I sure am sorry for getting drunk and fighting, no hard feelings, okay?

Uh, sure, they'd answer, do I know you? We ain't kin, are we?

2

*T*otaling a car and living to tell about it was a rite of passage. Several of my friends were killed in car wrecks around this time and another wished he had been. This last was Harrison Phillips, Bob's cousin. He was older, about Ronald J.'s age, slight and dark with a God-given sneer and wavy hair combed in a ducktail.

Back then people said they were going to shag when they meant leave or go somewhere, as in, I think I'll shag over to so-and-so's and get me some loving. To say the word *shag* was to be cool, and Harrison was very cool in his ducktail, leather jacket with upturned collar, a James Dean cigarette hanging loose, and driving a souped-up fifty-five Chevy Bel Air painted factory red and white and rolling on whitewall tires. Pretty soon everyone started calling him Shag instead of Harrison.

The roads of Logan County snaked along the mountainsides, often twisting back on themselves, diving under shelves of overhanging rock, or edging along sheer cliffs of fifty feet or more. It was customary to turn off the headlights at night to see if another car was coming at you around a curve, leaving a decision of whether to stay in your own lane at reasonable speed or pound it to the floor and take the whole road.

One night Shag was out worrying the hard pavement between Man and Logan, a mason jar of moonshine between his thighs, brain synapses stunned by the one-ninety proof. All was fine until he drifted past a curve and got air under him. That section dropped straight into the hollow below, and when they found him the next morning the headlight knob was pushed in. Shag had been running blind.

He survived, paralyzed from neck to toes. When he got home from the hospital we filed past as if viewing someone in a coffin. They had him stretched out on a device resembling an ironing board. All he could do was speak, and he said, Thanks for coming, fuckers, why are you looking at me? I want to die, just leave me the hell alone. So we did, all except Mama who went by and read to him, and a huge black miner named Chester who sometimes came after his shift and took him places.

One place they went was to Man High football games. Chester had made a chair out of wood that looked like a kid's car seat of today, but without the padding. Shag weighed practically nothing by this time, just a head mostly. When Chester lifted him up, he looked like a man carrying a puppet. You almost expected Chester to put his hand inside Shag's clothes and make his mouth and arms move.

Chester and Shag would sit together at the games, Shag strapped into his chair, Chester sometimes holding the mason jar to Shag's lips. In return for this kindness Shag treated Chester like shit.

Give me another drink, fuckhead, he'd say.

Chester might reply, Shag, son, watch your mouf, they kids and women here.

And Shag would answer, Shut up, Chester, I don't need no lame-ass telling me what to do.

Chester would look around and chuckle, saying, Ain't he something? Ain't that Shag something, though? Spunky, huh?

Then Shag was likely to say, Goddammit, I'm going to kick me some nigger ass if you don't pass that jar. I'm just about fed up with you. And this would drive Chester into spasms of laughter. Nobody thought Shag meant any of these insults. Everyone knew he loved Chester, truly loved him, and when he got drunk and cried it was Chester who dried his face and hugged him and said it was all okay and not to worry. Sometimes Chester cried too, tears streaming down that powerful face, hands like shovels swiping at them.

Vernon Simons had been a socially invisible slender boy with blonde hair and a big nose. He was one who didn't make it. On a spring night while sipping moonshine from a jar he took an outside curve too wide, gaining air astride the combustibles and torqued-out horses and dropping into a hollow with a noise like loud indifference. There was never a lot of Vernon to start with, and I suppose even less following the accident. At the service his family kept the coffin closed, although many of us had been curious to see what he looked like all broken up among the stuffed satin.

Vernon dead was more popular than Vernon alive, and a myth grew up around his brief and otherwise ordinary life, that of youth perishing in the sharp crush of steel. It confirmed those popular tunes where kids raced against trains or each other and died violently, usually sung in falsetto against heavenly background refrains. Sharon, also sixteen, had been Vernon's myopic and overfat girlfriend, and she prospered a few weeks on the sympathy. Air in front of the lockers at Man High was thick and humid with feminine sobbing. This also constituted a teen passage of sorts, elevating the surviving girlfriend to a status near widowhood.

It all fascinated Bob, who hadn't been particularly close to Vernon. The young have abbreviated memories, and Vernon quickly became mind haze except to Sharon, and later Bob, who started going over to Sharon's house and sitting on the sofa while she wept and told him stories of the attentive Vernon. Bob never said exactly what form these took, knowing we weren't interested. Sharon was actually a shrew, always yapping at Vernon to do this or that, and he had stood there and taken it. Larry and I figured he was just pussy-whipped. Bob's thoughts were somewhat different, and he told us that one of us needed to marry her, that it was the only way she could be protected.

Protected from what? we asked. Larry said he was prepared to eat shit first, maybe a bushel of it, which was my feeling exactly. We told Bob he was on his own. Bob got mad, which never made sense considering all three of us couldn't be married to the same girl. He told us to kiss his ass and thumbed over to Sharon's. That attitude didn't last long, and soon he was ogling other girls along with the rest of us, although never letting loose the notion that Sharon was now helpless.

In fact, three years later when they were nineteen the two of them got married and Daddy hired Bob to work in the lab at the mine, where he did jobs like measuring the pH of water with little strips of paper that changed color and then filling out forms that went off somewhere to be filed. Daddy said he was a good worker, never missed any days, and was glad to have given Bob a chance. Daddy had been leery at first, knowing he was my friend and therefore automatically a fuckup. I never knew the married Bob. By then I was gone.

Hardy Waynes, who lived up Nigger Holler, worked at the filling station in Man pumping gas and making oil changes. Hardy was about twenty-two and friendly. I liked seeing him, and sometimes we shot baskets together at the makeshift court at the end of the field behind our house. I was taller than Hardy, but he was stocky and strong, and playing against him was always a challenge. Hardy had dozens of squirrel tails hanging off his car antenna. He loved shooting squirrels and then eating them, fried or in a stew, and always kept a loaded squirrel gun in his trunk.

Everyone knew about the danger of smoking around gasoline, but Hardy didn't care. He filled your tank with a live butt hanging off his lower lip, then bent down close to be sure the gas cap was screwed on right. He often slopped gas on himself when pulling out the nozzle, and it was a miracle he never caught fire or blew himself up along with a customer.

We saw Hardy one night in the Smokehouse on going to shoot pool. Y'all ain't been in for gas lately, he said. We agreed that we hadn't. I guess what I mean is, you ain't been up to *buying* gas lately. I keep an eye on such things, he said, then grinned and shook our hands all around.

Hardy was right. At night we went to parking lots near the mines during mid-shift and siphoned a little gas from several vehicles so the owners wouldn't notice. The lots were never guarded, but we crept around anyway, hunching low and whispering. There was no purpose to buying gas when it was right there for free, but it seemed as if one of us was always tasting it later and making jokes about exhaling and then lighting up a cigarette.

This is how one eventful evening started. Larry was getting set to leave for boot camp and had a night job running the movie projector in Man, so Bob and I went without him. I had Daddy's Oldsmobile four-door sedan painted cream and coral, only about a year old. I think it was the first car Daddy had ever bought new. Be careful with my car, Daddy said when handing over the keys, no speeding or fooling around.

After filling up the tank at one of the mines, we stopped at a fry shack where a couple of girls we knew worked as waitresses. The owner didn't appreciate loiterers taking up paying space at his counter, so we ordered beers and fries. One of the girls started cozying up to Bob when she wasn't tossing plates of burgers off the arm, and they even swapped some spit during dry spells. Bob found this encouraging and wanted to stay. I had nowhere else to go, so we ordered two more beers and hung around.

After another couple each we slid off the stools saying we'd be back at closing and headed somewhere else, which proved to be another fry shack a few miles away. We had some beers and then it was time to pick up the girls. We were feeling good and talking about getting into a fight somewhere and kicking ass. I stopped for an old boy who was thumbing, telling him we'd drop him at our destination. He said that was fine with him and got in the backseat.

Let's honk this mother, Bob said. He was bouncing up and down on the seat trying to make himself go faster. I tromped the accelerator and humped it up to ninety, shutting off the headlights at the approach of every blind curve. The road was pretty much deserted, and I could take the inside as often as I wanted. Bob had maxed up the radio. The windows were fully open, the night rushing past my ears until all I heard was wind and the isolated note.

I hadn't given much thought to our location when suddenly a one-lane bridge came into view with another car just passing across it to the other side. I hit the brakes, sending us into a screeching slide, then instinctively twisted the wheel the other way. The Olds straightened out an instant before smashing head-on into the abutment.

At that moment I saw unforgiving gray steel yaw up and out of sight, the concrete wall coming on hard and flat and pockmarked, growing brighter in the headlights. I felt a terror powerful enough to swallow me whole. Forward velocity stopped abruptly with the sound of metal being shortened. Next came disorientation as the car rolled down the embankment and finally landed on its wheels in the creek. I remember the dashboard striking me hard in the chest, then I was careening off the ceiling and door and seat, and probably off Bob too. No seat belts in those days. The steering wheel had got shoved sideways and missed me completely, but the impact pushed the engine through the firewall. How our legs avoided being crushed was a miracle. Maybe it happened when our bodies were airborne.

I was shaking and even touched myself to be sure I could feel, unlike Shag. Christ, I thought, so this is real fear. I looked over at Bob, who was also sitting upright, although leaning a little crooked. Just moments before he'd stuck two unlit Pall Malls in his mouth intending to light one for each of us. They were bent but still there. He said, Want me to push the lighter in?

Our lives, spent mostly in pursuit of comfort and attachment to boredom, can achieve spectacular definition only during a few seconds of terror. We sat there as the black water rose to our waists and laughed until tears sprang out and every breath was a sickly gasp. We kept howling even as the hitchhiker put his shoulder to the crumpled door and fell with it into the creek; even when he stood and said, Y'all are crazy as hell, and scrambled up the bank to the hard road and ran away into the darkness. Suddenly we reverted to what we really were: tired, drunk, and wet as muskrats. Eventually we crawled out through the windows and thumbed home.

I arrived at the house in the early morning still trailing remnants of creek water. Everyone was asleep, but I went into my parents' bedroom and woke up Daddy. He was cross. What the hell do you want? he asked. I wrecked the car, I said. When he didn't say anything more I went to bed.

Later, dressed for work, Daddy shook me awake. Where's the Olds?

I told you last night, I wrecked it, I replied.

Yeah, but where is it?

I hit a bridge, and it's in the middle of a creek.

There was silence while Daddy considered this news.

So that means you totaled it?

I guess so, I answered.

Well, you son of a bitch, he said, and belted me in the head. You son of a bitch. And he walked away and slammed the door.

That afternoon Daddy and the insurance man went to see the car for themselves. Then the insurance man called a tow truck to come pull it out of the creek and take it to a junkyard.

The next day Daddy and I had our only father-son talk. He came into my room and sat down on the bed while I stood nervously by the door. He put his elbows on his knees and made a steeple out of his fingers and looked at me hard. This was different from other times when I screwed up and he whipped off his belt and let me have it. I never resented any of those occasions, having earned every one of them. But this time I was truly nervous. He looked thoughtful, as if deciding how to explain to a dog why it had to quit shitting on the rug.

This isn't the first time I ever missed work because of your pure stupidity, he said. And it damn well better be the last. I said yessir and tried to look suitably ashamed. Furthermore, he continued, I know you're smoking and drinking and otherwise carrying on and ignoring school and that girls are probably involved too. You've just turned seventeen. First boarding school and now this. Is it all part of a plan or are you just following your dick around? I mumbled something about straightening out and doing better in school. I didn't mention having not attended classes for the past few weeks, figuring it might be what some call an inopportune moment. He shook his head in disgust and stalked out, leaving behind a bleak aura of disaster.

It's true I was a disappointment to my parents, who had only my best interests in mind. My family was kind. I loved them and felt genuine remorse while knowing deep inside that nothing would change. It was the continuation of distancing myself for no apparent reason, opening a chasm that widened with passing years until Jane became like an only child, and even she and I rarely saw each other or spoke on the phone. I lay a while on the bed feeling guilty, then walked down the train tracks to refill the water jugs and have a smoke. Despite the bad timing I was thinking about girls.

After the story of the accident spread, suitably embellished by Bob, the girls started getting even friendlier, although I wasn't driving around retrieving any of them. Daddy had replaced the car, but he left me traveling by thumb, which meant I sometimes didn't make it home.

On one occasion Larry, Bob, and I were hanging around in front of the Smokehouse with some others when Bill Bostick the constable pulled up. We started teasing Bill as usual, pounding on the hood of his car and saying unkind things about the parentage of those who labor in law enforcement, but this night he was in no mood.

Get in, he said.

We didn't do nothing yet, said a kid named Alvin.

No, but you're liable to. I got a cold and ain't about to be woke up at three ayem of the morning to chase after you. Now get in.

Bill took us to jail where we spent the night among drifters from the trains and snoring drunks sleeping it off on black lung disability. The next morning Bill opened early then took us for coffee at the Smokehouse. He said he felt better after a good night's sleep, and that he had us to thank for it.

At boarding school I had started thinking in a modest way about intellectual pursuits. The symbol system of mathematics, presented to students as problems to be solved, was interesting in short doses or when applied to a purpose, but I never liked puzzles for the sake of solving them. A career in poetry seemed far more exciting than pushing a slide rule and hoping for the right outcome. The incipient engineers and mathematicians I later knew in college had more trouble getting laid than a dog missing its hind legs, but poets reputedly had lots of women, at least those who weren't overtly queer or completely dysfunctional. Although I read and appreciated poems and even tried writing some lines, I was deficient in certain emotional and mental attributes, including high levels of dramatic sensibility.

No poet can be taken seriously without displaying acute dementia and other antisocial tendencies. For example, I never had nightmares populated by dead writers like the autobiographical young men in Roberto Bolaño's stories, nor was I plagued by what Jim Harrison calls the poet's overdeveloped consciousness. Hart Crane's outsized sentiment eluded me completely, but it helped knowing that at the end he carefully folded his coat and left it on the ship's railing before jumping overboard. My days and nights lacked that loathsome feeling described by Thomas

Hardy of being a ghost among his surroundings, degraded to the point of invisibility. Barry Hannah's requirements of indirectness, poorly developed senses, and a faulty memory also fell beyond my grasp. In fact, my only qualifications for writing poetry were exceptional drinking capacity and an abiding and unsavory horniness, neither of which actually causes printed words to appear. This last pronouncement is scarcely a revelation, Charles Bukowski and others having laid earlier claim.

I finally understood that to poets drinking and other diversions represented ways of killing time while awaiting inspiration. Then it occurred to me, why waste a perfectly good night's drinking by fabricating some paltry excuse over art? The situation was straightforward: any activity that diluted the capacity to concentrate lengthened the distance between art and its completion. Poets, in other words, might do better if they stayed sober. After figuring this out I said to hell with it, I'm not ready to concentrate that intensely.

Science, however, opened a whole different vista. Brief periods of heavy task-oriented thinking can culminate in results nearly proportionate with effort, unlike art in any form, which requires endless attention and can still leave you deeply empty. On a cost-benefit basis the study of science proved far simpler. At the end of a hard day in the lab or in the field you went home, popped a beer, and flipped on the teevee like anyone else, but better not try this if you hoped to be an artist of any kind.

I stopped thinking about poetry at seventeen and turned to biology, an older, more visceral love. Mr. Henshaw, the shop teacher at Man Junior High, cracked open a door when he had ordered us into the woods to retrieve leaves from trees representing the different materials we were using. I remember him listing maple, hickory, oak (white and red), yellow poplar, pine, spruce, and black walnut. The consequences of not following through were dire, and there was panic when nobody could find a black walnut tree until a kid thought there might be one growing in his coal camp and collected enough leaves for us all.

Observation often precedes knowledge, and after that experience I began actually looking at the trees when I went into the woods. With the help of a field guide I soon learned to recognize the major species and switched to the lesser ones. It was satisfying, and I tested myself in autumn when the deciduous specimens were bare and looked similar. This led to an examination of growth forms and barks as a way of distinguishing one from another. Wildflowers came next. I often stopped beside the road to examine a flowering weed, walked into pastures at a flash of distant color, and haunted shady glens and stream banks. Before long I had acquired a workable knowledge of the Appalachian flora. My friends found this behavior curious but seemed disinclined to ridicule it. Even if they had it wouldn't have mattered.

Plants were fascinating, but so were animals. When I was very young we lived far out in the country in a small house—a cabin, actually—without electricity. Mama got well water from a hand pump on the kitchen counter. Jane was a baby, and to bathe us Mama heated water in pans set atop the coal stove and poured it into a washtub on the floor.

There was an outhouse to the left of the front door and a tool shed straight ahead where Daddy kept his tools. He allotted me a couple of shelves I could reach, and Mama provided some empty jars with lids. Using a hammer and nail I punched holes in the lids to let in air, then caught spiders to imprison. I first dropped two sticks into a jar and crossed them, making a lattice where webs could be attached. A newly captured spider crawled frantically around the bottom of the jar, but within a day it usually spun a web and then hung upside down waiting for food. I never thought it mattered to a spider whether it lived in a corner of an old barn or in a jar. I fed my spiders by stunning flies with a flyswatter and dropping them onto the webs. It was always better if they had a little twitch left in them.

But my real love was water and the things living in it. A creek flowed past the house. It was shallow and clear in summer, and I spent most of my time alone in it catching crawfish and aquatic insect larvae, which I kept alive in buckets by changing some of the water daily. I learned to move upstream to keep from ruining the visibility, and to turn over the flat stones slowly so as not to panic any creature lurking underneath. Daddy got a little net somewhere, and I sometimes captured a minnow or darter for my buckets. Stonefly nymphs and panting minnows moved through my dreams, their noses pressed to creek rocks, eyes protruded like the navels of certain oranges.

I also kept snakes, salamanders, and frogs in different containers, whatever was available, but these were less interesting than the fishes and crawfish, which were always in motion. In spring a box turtle inevitably blundered across the yard. Daddy would drill a tiny hole at the very back edge of its shell through which I tied a long string. I tied the other end to a tree that leaned over the creek. I fed the turtle vegetables and earthworms, and it could go to the creek for water. For two years running I caught turtles with holes in their shells, indicating they hadn't traveled very far after being released.

In late summer there were mantids. I once found a small brown preying mantis and put it on the trunk of a tree where it was camouflaged perfectly. I fed it a grasshopper now and then, and it stayed in the same spot for probably two weeks. And every summer there was at least one mole or shrew huddled morosely in a wooden box filled with earth and grass. The moles were black and velvety, the shrews smaller and gray, and both species usually starved despite my frantic search for earthworms. In autumn, just after school started, Mama made me release all the animals, even the spiders, saying they needed time to find homes and get settled for winter.

That shed, creek, and land all around were heaven. I had no need of playmates, having already been imprinted on wildlife, and my social development was arrested forever. If I was invited to a party, Mama always ended up apologizing to the other mothers because I left the group immediately to explore a field or step into a creek to turn over the rocks. The silence and joy of simply being alone outdoors were more satisfying than social interactions, and that has never changed.

Daddy planted a large garden one summer and strung a fence around it to keep out rabbits and woodchucks. Even so, something kept eating the new corn right on the cob without even breaking any stalks. Whatever it was peeled aside the husk and nibbled the kernels off cleanly from tip to stem leaving only the cob. The mystery continued unsolved until late one night when Daddy went to the outhouse and heard a noise in the garden. He got down on all fours, crept over to the fence, and there in the moonlight stood Tuppy, my dog, on her hind legs, front legs in the air not even trying to brace herself, chewing corn from a cob. After that we tied her up at night until the season for corn was over.

Daddy told that story for years. Ever hear of a dog eating corn? he would ask people. When they answered in the negative, he'd say, Well, my son had a dog once with a taste for corn. Ate it right off the cob and then left the cob on the stalk. Must have jumped the fence. Had me fooled for the longest time. Damndest thing I ever saw.

Once Mama was walking to the outhouse and saw a blacksnake, a black racer. I was by the tool shed, and she yelled for me to bring a hoe saying there was a big snake and she needed to kill it. Instead of the hoe I picked up a wooden box and carried it out to her, tripping and falling over it and barking my shins. She was keeping an eye on the snake, which was lying in the grass sunning itself, and hadn't noticed what I was doing. I said, Here, Mama, we can catch it in this box, but she insisted on killing it, so I ran and got the hoe. This made me sad because I wanted to catch that snake and study it. Mama felt uncomfortable around big snakes, although she tolerated small ones if I kept them confined in the tool shed.

I have one other memory of that place, or maybe Mama told me the story years later. When you go back that far the recollections two people have of a single event become stuck together like sheets of old paper, and when you pull them apart each leaves some of itself on the other. I can still picture a little church backed up to a courtyard surrounded by a low wall. Mama made me sit through Sunday school while the adults attended service inside. A room for kids was available, but in warm weather they took us out to the courtyard to be inculcated. It was spring, and I was wearing new shoes and trousers and a new jacket. The courtyard wall had been freshly whitewashed, and during the instruction I escaped over it and into a nearby creek. After church Mama came out and found me. She asked if I'd enjoyed Sunday school, and I said that I had. I was standing knee-deep in muddy creek water still wearing my shoes and socks and trousers, the front of my jacket white with dried lime from the wall. I pulled a salamander from my pocked and showed it to her.

    I remember Mama laughing and reaching down for my hand.

3

Cap had somehow survived the March 1959 purge at the boy's dorm when ten of us were expelled from West Nottingham Academy. Our personal surveillance system devised to monitor faculty meetings failed at a crucial moment. Installing the system required drilling a tiny hole in the ceiling of the conference room to hide a microphone and then extending the necessary cables from the mike to a tape recorder owned by another student who lived in a room directly above. Access to the conference room had become possible when Cap and some others acquired a master key for an hour or so and filed a duplicate.

Everything had been fine until then. A select few of us knew exactly when the raids were scheduled, providing ample time to hide our illegal liquor and cigarettes. And we also found out when extra security patrols were scheduled that could interfere with nocturnal visits to Rowland Hall where the girls lived. I had a girlfriend there, and Cap had several.

It was easy to climb into the windows of the girls' dorm and just as easy for them to climb out. The master key fit the backdoor to the chapel, and late at night a few of us were also getting laid on its pews under a disapproving stained-glass Jesus. We thought of these sins as minor, syncopated as they were with God's own cosmic rhythms. Life was good.

Cap and I mostly stopped going to class in early spring. I started taking long showers instead of attending the morning sessions and thought about where this aimlessness might be leading. I recognized dimly how the anointed had mastered art and science while the rest picked up cans and bottles along state roads or toiled a lifetime in public education. It was metaphysical angst, and I was trying to turn it over like a creek rock and peer underneath. The communal shower had several heads. After aiming them all at one corner I sat naked on the floor under the cascade. One morning Cap joined me. He aimed half the heads at the opposite corner and sat down too. It was pleasant just hanging out, and occasionally we moved away from the water and had a smoke.

Once as we were lighting up, Mr. Casale, who taught history, stepped in. He was a former Marine drill instructor, and he was also smoking a butt. He said, You've both run out of demerits. I could have your asses tossed for smoking in the showers, but I won't. Watch me. He bent his lower lip inward and the cigarette disappeared into his mouth. He ducked under one of the shower heads, soaped up from head to toe, and rinsed down. Then he popped the cigarette back out, still hanging on his lower lip, and took a drag without touching it. If you insist on being fuckups, he told us as he grabbed his towel, learn to do it right.

Mr. Casale's sudden appearance rattled us, not from any fear of retribution but because he had labeled us fuckups. He was right, of course, according to the student conduct code, but something else was in play, something undefined and niggling just under the skin. Today neither Cap nor I can recall whether he gave it to me or I to him, but we passed Jack Kerouac's novel *On the Road* back and forth, suddenly discovering answers to questions we had been too inarticulate or inexperienced to ask. The book profoundly affected us. In truth it changed our lives.

No other writer of the fifties nailed down his generation as Kerouac had defined the Beats. It all began with a borderline Catholic mysticism: by Kerouac's definition somebody "beat" possessed a scrofulous holy aura, perhaps being blessed with Aquinas' beatific vision or whatever humble parts of it might be accessible to the living. No coincidence, "beatific" and "beat." A Beat was cool, an outsider "beaten down" by life and circumstance and too tired and jaded to care: man, I'm beat, you know?

The literature on tangential paths has a long history, some of which I had already read, one example being Colin Wilson's *The Outsider*, published in 1956. But it was Kerouac who stripped away the academic trappings and made everything clear, or so we thought back then. We were tragic, not fuckups, and we broke rules because they seemed irrelevant, not out of spite, a predilection for rule breaking, or to draw attention to ourselves. The notion of going along to get along—of living by an artificial code—was repugnant and dishonest. The freakish energy of Kerouac's writing masked a compelling simplicity: be true to yourself, seek new experiences, listen to the music, and *live*. Basically, he said, screw what everyone else might do or say. Follow your instincts, and if you don't then you deserve to be rendered deaf and mute and consigned to the accounting profession. The camouflaged answer had lain in front of us all along: although the outside world is large and often unnerving, there's no excuse for living small inside yourself.

*R*amon Naranjo, hip denizen of Santo Domingo, broke a leg playing basketball. At midnight I carried him piggyback down the dormitory fire escape, then down the ladder at the bottom, plastered appendage dangling off to one side like a pale malignancy.

I'm embarrassed, he whispered, accent strong on vowels, forehead caressed by a black curl. Ramon the Latin Elvis, snow nibbling at the dusky toes sticking out of that cast leg among rumors of warm Caribbean nights. *Coño*, man, this hurts, man, *la escalera*, I mean . . . the fucking ladder . . . *ow, ow*, my cast!

There's no humiliation, only dedication, I whispered back, huffing under his weight and the night's blank translucence.

We hobbled across the field to Rowland Hall under a starry sky where it took my girlfriend and her roomie each pulling one arm and me pushing from outside to shoehorn Ramon's fat cast and scrawny ass through the window.

*I*t could never have lasted. In March someone ratted me out, not Ramon but me. Someone with a grudge, no doubt. It's true that my demeanor had pissed off some people, students and faculty both. I was called before the disciplinary committee of the administration.

You're in big trouble, the Headmaster said, if you don't name the girl.

What girl? I replied.

You're going to be expelled anyway, so might as well name the girl, said one of the teachers.

If I'm being expelled anyway, why should I? Besides, I don't know what you're talking about.

You were sneaking into Rowland Hall.

I don't remember doing that.

The survivors briefly mourned my passing, Cap told me later, and immediately moved some booze into the empty room, my roomie Moose having been expelled the month before.

*T*wo months later, in mid-May and after totaling Daddy's car, I hopped a bus out of Man for Pottsville, Pennsylvania, and stayed with Cap a couple of days. We spent most of that time in the colored whorehouses along Minersville Street reprising our better boarding school memories. Cap's older brother Joe was already at the beach where he had a job lined up as a lieutenant of the Long Beach Island Township, New Jersey, lifeguards. Cap had worked as a guard the year before and said I could get a job too. I had the necessary qualifications—lifesaving certificates from both the Red Cross and YMCA—but still needed a Social Security card. I ended up working there as a guard for four straight summers.

We left Pottsville in Joe's car, a fifty-four blue Ford coupe, and drove to Beach Haven where Joe and two of his buddies had rented a place in town. It turned out to be a former gift shop directly on Bay Avenue, the main thoroughfare bisecting the skinny length of Long Beach Island, and built in the shape of a log with a door in the middle. It even had fake bark on the outside. Inside, the walls curved inward like those of a sailboat, and only the floor and ceiling were flat. There was room for six iron cots. The place was owned by a couple named AJ and Betty who had an ice cream shop next door called AJ's.

Cap and I went over to pay the first week's rent, about ten bucks each, and meet the landlord. Betty, a weary blonde, was on her knees scrubbing the floor attended by a bucket of soapy water while AJ sat at the counter reading the racing form. He set down the paper long enough to glance at us and take our money.

Inside the Log we greeted Joe and met Henny and Ray. Joe was a little taller than Cap and had dark hair and olive skin. No one would ever suspect they were brothers. Henny was a collegiate football player, huge and genial and bald, Mr. Clean's doppelgänger without the earring. Ray, Henny's best buddy, was as small as Henny was large. All three guys were majoring in physical education, and their conversations were mostly about jock stuff. There was no toilet or shower or even running water. We took to shitting in the vacant lot in back and showering with a garden hose attached to AJ's.

The next day I found the post office and filled out a Social Security form. The minimum age for lifeguarding was eighteen, so I lied and made myself a year older. Cap and I went to the township police station and applied for lifeguard jobs, although the beaches were not scheduled to open officially for three weeks. I told the clerk I would fill in my Social Security number later, that I had lost the card.

Meanwhile we needed money. Joe got a job painting a motel. There was lots of scraping, and the owner hired Cap and me and put us to work. It might have paid enough to cover food and rent but only lasted a couple of days because Joe fell off the roof. It was just one storey and Joe wasn't hurt, but the owner fired us anyway.

I saw in the classifieds that a dairy in Toms River on the mainland needed milkmen, so I borrowed Joe's car and went over and applied. They said I could start at three o'clock the next morning.

They put me in a white uniform and a white hat with a rolled brim and told me to accompany the driver and memorize the route. He was a middle-aged guy dressed in the same uniform and bore a resemblance to Barney Fife of Mayberry: thin and nervous with bug eyes and an Adam's apple that was hard not to look at. He seemed happy having someone to boss around. He said things like, Now you take a bottle of homogenized up to Miz Norton's and leave it on the porch and hurry right back, we got us a whole route to run and there can't be no screwing off. Always remember, you need to finish up by nine ayem, hear me? Son, are you listening? And I nodded and said yessir. And I ain't going to be here helping you after Friday 'cause I got me a new route. You'll have this one all to yourself. Be careful of them bottles you're carrying and don't let them clank around.

It took two days learning where to leave what and check it off on a clipboard. There was an order for three homogenized and a butter here, a pasteurized and pint of whipping cream there. We also carried bread and rolls but nothing frozen like ice cream. Then you returned to the dairy where you handed in the clipboard, did inventory of the truck with a clerk, took off the uniform and hung it up, and went home. I was finished when most people were just getting to work.

The truck was insulated and carried ice, more than enough to keep all the dairy products cold so long as you didn't leave the door open. You pulled up to the curb, put the stick in neutral, and yanked the hand brake. Then you jumped out of the seat, ducked into the back, put the order in a wire basket, and bounced up to the front door. Hardly anyone was awake until late in the run when you might see a few scraggly housewives or a bleary-eyed guy in robe and slippers fishing the newspaper out of his bushes.

I had been working a couple of weeks when Joe said he needed the car earlier than I normally got back. I told the dispatcher that I no longer had a ride. She said, Okay, take the truck home after inventory, but be here by two ayem so we can load it, and I can't pay you for that extra hour. I said fine. The first morning after work when I parked the truck in front of the Log, Henny came out and said, Cool, we're having a party tonight and need someplace to keep the beer cold. I said there was still plenty of ice, and we got in the truck and went off to buy beer.

That was the Log's christening. Joe knew lots of people, and our place was so full you couldn't turn around. There was a houseful of girls from Pennsylvania living around the corner, and all of them came. The party spilled into the yard about the same time we ran out of beer, so Joe and I took the truck and picked up a keg. I backed the truck up to the Log and opened the rear doors so the keg was accessible. At two in the morning the party was still going strong and I was drunk.

The cops came and asked whose party it was, and we said ours. Are you guys twenty-one? they asked. When nobody answered, one of the cops said, Okay, then who bought the beer for you?

It was Eddy Knauss, Cap spoke up. Eddie bought it.

The cop took out a notebook. Is that Knauss with a K and one s or just an N with one s or two?

Cap looked thoughtful. Yeah, I think so, he said.

Which? the cop asked.

I think with a K and at least two esses, but you don't say the K out loud.

The cop wrote it down. Where's this Mr. Knauss at present? he asked.

I couldn't tell you, Cap said. We were told to break it up.

Won't Eddy get in trouble? a girl whispered to Cap.

Naw, he told her, Eddy died in high school. Car wreck, very bloody and awful. As I recall he was decapitated at both neck and scrotum.

That's so sad, the girl said.

I know, Cap said, I could sure use a little comforting right now.

About noon a cop knocked on the door and said that a dairy had called to report its milk truck missing and a patrol had spotted it in our yard. We had all been asleep. I explained how it wasn't stolen, that I was simply late for work. Cap got up and followed me over to Toms River in Joe's car, at which point I was given my pay and promptly fired. That's a relief, said Cap. Now we can go back and get some sleep. I've got a helluva headache.

On a night in mid-July a police patrol spotted Ray and Henny soaping up and hosing each other off on the front lawn. The cops asked what the hell was this, taking showers naked with a garden hose right on the main street. Shit flows downhill, and on finding out we had no facilities they notified the health department, which issued a warning to AJ, who evicted us. Joe, Henny, and Ray moved in with friends.

I don't recall how Cap and I found the Evelyn House, a huge white boarding house on Liberty Avenue just south of Beach Haven. No one we knew lived there. Too much time has passed, and Cap can't remember either. It was run full-time by Evelyn Keating with occasional help from her husband and married daughter who had jobs elsewhere and were mostly around on weekends. Johnny Keating, Mrs. Keating's youngest, was also a full-time summer resident. He was thirteen that first year and precocious, taking every advantage of our attempts to corrupt him. The place was segregated into separate sections for girls and boys, mostly college students working summer jobs. Mrs. Keating, through tireless Catholic zeal, did her best to keep the genders apart, but some spillover was inevitable.

Cap and I started out renting a room with a double bed on the second floor. The bathroom was down the hall. The outside of the house was being repainted, and there was a ladder leaning against the wall outside our room. I had met an adventurous dark-haired girl from Philadelphia named Rachel who often visited the beach I guarded to chat about poetry. Her family came from money. She was an English major at some expensive Midwestern college, older than I and very sophisticated. I mentioned my new address, and a night or two later she climbed the ladder and crawled through the window. We fucked until morning when she got dressed and climbed back out. This went on regularly. Cap, who was often trying to sleep in the same bed, was being driven crazy. Wherever the ladder ended up after a day's painting I waited until dark and moved it back underneath our window. Eventually the job was finished and our trysts shifted to the beach up the street.

Rachel and I saw each other irregularly over three summers and corresponded during the winters, always discussing our common interest in literature. I was, she wrote, her "soul mate," the only person who accepted her as she was and shared a common interest.

I phoned her in Philadelphia prior to leaving for the beach in 1961. It was May and she was just home from college, having graduated a week or so previously. I said I would be coming to Philly by train and taking a bus to Beach Haven and could we maybe get together. She had a playful personality. I'm not sure, she giggled, who is this again?

Why not? I asked.

Because I'm engaged and getting married in August. It's one of those big goddamn weddings. My mother is planning it, of course, like she plans everything in my life. Every Jew in Philly is invited. Rachel hadn't mentioned a boyfriend. There was a large silence before she said, Okay, I'll pick you up at the train station. I told her when I was getting in.

She collected me in a Mercedes smelling of new leather, having told her parents about visiting a girlfriend over the weekend. She wore a print dress and a smile, but had thoughtfully left the engagement ring at home. We checked into a motel and fucked for two days, surfacing now and then to eat at an always-open diner across the street. The fiancé never came up in conversation. I pictured him as ordinary and studious in appearance and wearing a yarmulke, probably a lawyer or accountant, maybe a businessman. He read the *Wall Street Journal*, not John Donne, *Business Week* instead of Dylan Thomas, certainly not "Howl," that contemporary bohemian polemic written by a fellow Jew.

In her impending married life Rachel would be held in a passive web of expensive objects, holidays, parties, children in private schools, extended family, the synagogue. Women of her status had few options. Only in relative poverty can true choices exist. She knew this already, as I learned when she drove me to the bus station and kissed me goodbye. I was turning to open the door when she touched my arm and said, Wait, look at me. She put a hand against my cheek and studied my face a minute, as if memorizing it. The dark brown of her eyes blended perfectly with the rich upholstery, the genuine wood paneling on the dash, the elegant fingernails and diamond earrings.

I'm really going to miss you, she said, and started to cry. I never saw her or heard her voice again.

*O*ur next room at the Evelyn House was even smaller, although still furnished with a chair and double bed. It was all we could afford. Cap and I slept facing away from each other and threw our dirty clothes in a pile against the wall. Then Uncle Dirty moved in with us and Mrs. Keating put a cot crosswise at the end of the bed. The rule was that whoever came in last slept on the clothes, which were probably cleaner than the bed. They were definitely less sandy. If you came in late it was usually okay because Cap would be shacked up with a girl who rented the next room. Her bed was just on the other side of the wall and the proximity and consistent banging of the headboard was a natural sleep aid, similar to raindrops on a barn roof.

Mrs. Keating, nervous by nature, became distraught. The three of us couldn't live in filth like this, not in her house, she said, it was unsanitary. We admitted to sloth and ignorance, but emphasized poverty. After consulting her husband she emptied out the attic, furnished it with cots, and let us move up there for eight dollars a week each. The attic was bisected by steep stairs down to the third floor where the bathroom was. There were single double-hung windows at each end of the room for light, and the ceiling and walls were unfinished wood. At night we had a bare bulb with a pull chain. Mrs. Keating supplied a floor fan, but with none of the house air conditioned all the heat rose to our section. On windless days it was nearly unbearable. Even so the attic soon filled with other boarders. Don Hicks crashed there off and on when he wanted a break from sleeping in his car. There were others over that first summer and those following whose names and faces I don't remember, mostly pustulant young men who arrived wet-combed and looking newly paroled.

Roy Holly stands out, a paranoid schizophrenic and vicious street fighter who self-medicated with alcohol. Roy was a curator of slights and small hatreds, a bearer of everlasting grudges. His parents lived somewhere nearby, and when things at home got shaky they eased him onto the street and covered the eight bucks a week it cost to live with us, plus enough spending cash to keep the buzz going. Roy must have been thirty or so. He spoke a peculiar language, not pidgin exactly but not standard English either. For example, I took showers, but Roy tipped to the rain room to cop some dew. These phrases were uttered in a rush of words, the more recent clambering over those still hanging in the air. Roy seldom slept, dissolving instead into bouts of hallucinatory twilight punctuated by screams as hordes of imaginary spiders spun webs to trap his consciousness. Nights were the worst, times of blackness and sorrow when the moon looked like a gouged eye and we heard him crawling slowly up the stairs bloodied and shouting reprisals of real or imagined insults, sometimes pausing to puke.

The stairs were an inconvenience when you had to take a leak, so we started pissing out one of the windows. Mrs. Keating's marigolds along that side of the house withered and died despite the heroic efforts of herself and her daughter. It became a horticultural puzzle much discussed in the Keating family. Books about gardening were obtained from the library and there was talk of unbalanced soil pH and likely nutrient impairment, especially phosphorus, a required something for photosynthesis, which in turn had something to do with light. Mr. Keating held forth that, in his opinion, the previous summer having been sunnier than the present one offered sufficient evidence of a light deficiency, and dead marigolds could be part of a natural cycle. Only Johnny knew the real reason. He kept his mouth shut fearing we might quit giving him beer.

The window as urinal imprinted on Uncle D. a peculiar nocturnal pattern. This evidently took root as a lesion etched onto the primitive brain, that part held over from days when our ancestors fought over the choicest ants and nobody thought much about where he urinated. UD, arriving home shitfaced and stunned as a mole in the noontime sun, would reach the top of the stairs before pausing in apparent concentration. Evidently believing himself to be standing at the open window he unzipped his fly and pissed mightily. Actually he had stopped at the foot of his own cot. The rest of us put down our books or paused in the middle of passing weed and watched, fascinated.

After emptying the bladder (which in adult humans can hold three-fourths of a liter) he climbed onto his soggy mattress and slept like a baby, awaking the next morning only to shout, You bastards! Which one of you pissed in my bed? From animal studies we know that imprintation lasts a lifetime. Years later in our collective geezerhood UD confessed to Cap and me that as a forty-something and pole-axed by alcohol he occasionally repeated this maneuver using his wife's lingerie drawer. At the time of the story he no longer had a wife.

Although personable and not bad looking, Uncle Dirty was possessed of a sensitivity peculiar to abused pilgrims, those faithful who stoop in abnegation to better allow the lesser of our species, selfish women in particular, to dump on them. Oddly this genetic anomaly failed to keep him from abusing others, as manifested in laziness, lying, relentless mooching, and unrepentant amnesia toward personal debt. He claimed to abjure extravagance while wallowing in good food and drink at the first opportunity. And yet he seemed so naïve in his frailty and lied to us with such élan that we embraced him.

It was the halting vulnerability in his eyes, I suppose—large and brown, trusting, innocent as a leg-trapped fawn's—although eyes are bequeathed and develop apart from either strength or weakness. The window on the soul is opaque; what we see in someone's eyes is just the reflection back, your own soul laminated with illusion. This was never more apparent than near the end of his life when throat cancer was strangling him. His face had become narrow in pain and old age, but those remarkable eyes remained unchanged.

That was April 2007 when Cap and I dragged UD to Key West for a last hurrah, and he confessed to lifelong preferences for small breasts and cheap gin. We listened to his stories at a nude outdoor bar, moving with the shade as the sun moved. The days passed, and we became ever more wasted. Cap and I thought we could see the apparition of UD's cancer levitate beside him, but maybe it was only the sinuous smoke from his peculiar skinny cigarettes.

What the hell did it matter? UD would be dead by mid-July. He had tall white evangelist hair with just enough wave to confirm God's abhorrence of the straight line, and during our week together he used a blow dryer to keep it looking holy. In the motel room he kept a glass of straight rum beside the bed and sipped from it, anything to kill the pain. He was also popping Percocet, Valium, and Vicodin lubricated with cheap-gin martinis, beer chasers, and cocaine. He ate very little that week, existing mainly on cocktail onions and the calories from booze. With his motor running on ethanol UD was a credit to the government's corn subsidy.

*I*n that summer of 1959 Cap and I met Uncle D. for the first time on the deck of an outdoor bar that fronted Barnegat Bay. It was happy hour but we were already lit, having been drinking since noon. With us was Prattie, a friend of Joe's whose goal was to collect all his little hatreds into one large one. Prattie turned mean with alcohol and found the world contemptible, I believe, because most of its inhabitants were taller. Height envy is a curious thing considering that hominids learned to walk upright only in recent biological time, and that tallness offers no discernible advantage in terms of evolutionary fitness. Whatever gave Prattie his rotten attitude, we never liked each other, a feeling solidified after his girlfriend took up with me during one of his extended absences. They eventually reconnected and resumed courting. Following the usual interval of mindless rapture they married, produced children, and inflicted on each other condign suffering.

That afternoon, for reasons unknown, I jumped off the deck. The tide was low, the water about seven feet deep. It felt refreshing, so I stayed and splashed around while people peered over the rail and laughed. Upon ducking under I heard a discordant orchestra of a hundred tubas puffing the same note with monotonous enthusiasm. Without a face mask there was no hope of seeing anything. Directional hearing underwater is nearly impossible, and anyway the sound came from everywhere.

I swam to the bottom and groped around feeling only slime-covered beer glasses, but each contained something that squirmed when touched. I took a glass to the surface and saw an oyster toadfish inside. The fish had folded its tail partway over and backed in with its ugly flat head facing out. It was a stout little fish and filled the entire glass. The symphony down below comprised males serenading females. This was love's season for the oyster toadfish. Subsequent surface dives gave evidence of a thriving tenement of unbroken glasses each containing a toadfish jacked on hormones. Then Prattie jumped over the rail followed by Cap and the investigation ended. Soon there were dozens of revelers cooling off, some still holding their cocktails now diluted with muddy bay water.

Uncle D. was not among them, having missed the spectacle because he was at the bar arguing with this girlfriend. When I climbed back onto the deck I saw the girl thrashing on the floor. She was blonde and well tanned, and UD was trying to drag her down the stairs and away from there by her hair. After the bartenders intervened she departed alone. We introduced ourselves, and he stuck around. He told us he was a lifeguard moonlighting a second job as a bar waiter at the Baldwin Hotel. He said it was like stealing money on weekends when there was live entertainment. Like us, he was underage and not even supposed to be near liquor much less serving it.

The details of that lovers' quarrel emerged eventually. Unknown to UD, his girl, whose name was Nancy, had been stepping out on the sly with Joe. And unknown to Joe, his own love was meeting furtively with UD. These facts came together one day while Joe and UD were sitting together on the lifeguard stand.

Joe mentioned his girl's name but said he was secretly seeing a blonde called Nancy who had a jealous boyfriend. UD then noted that his girl was a blonde Nancy and he was seeing a brunette called so-and-so when no one was looking, who by coincidence had the same name as Joe's girl and from his description could have been her twin, and so forth.

In the end there was no animosity, although UD never got over the loss of Nancy. He grieved a lifetime. While dying of cancer he went to see Nancy and her husband in Philadelphia and stayed with them several days. During the Key West sojourn he told Cap and me that the visit had affected him greatly in a way he was unable to explain.

4

That fall of 1959 UD quit Rutgers University, found a menial job in New York, and began studying music with the aim of becoming a jazz musician. By the next summer he had quit the job, moved to the Evelyn House with Cap and me, and was taking lessons on flute and tenor sax.

It was UD who introduced us to the bohemian world, what we had been seeking all along. He taught us to smoke marijuana, which in those days carried a heavy prison sentence if you were caught. We met his acquaintances, most of them older by ten years or so, men and women working in shipyards, waiting tables, tending bar, guarding beaches, crewing on charter boats. They lived loosely with few possessions, often sharing quarters for the summer then scattering to the winter warmth of California, Florida, or Mexico. It was life on the drift, life *on the road*. The scholarly among them had read Wittgenstein, Kafka, Hesse, the Beats, and we hung out with them drinking beer and blowing weed and discussing philosophy, living as they lived in poverty and freedom. At least that's how it seemed to us. Ragged paperbacks passed hand to hand, and anyone with something to say made notes in the margins and left his initials for subsequent discussion, praise, or ridicule.

That summer of 1960 UD was driving a gray forty-nine Mercury coupe with an engine that sounded like liquid butter flowing over itself. Twice a week he left Beach Haven for Greenwich Village and his private music lessons, paid for by unemployment. I went along occasionally if I had the day off and napped on benches or passed the time among drooling junkies, prevaricating poets, earnest doomsayers, and the merely ignorant and sniveling. They were Bohemia's heirs and the new outsiders, Kerouac's subterraneans. As a participant there was little required except to stand around watching and listening and staying stoned. A decade earlier on these same streets Ronald Sukenick had uncovered the veridical appeal of simply doing nothing. He wrote, Drinking helps, so do drugs, but at its most refined hanging out is a form of meditation.

It was true.

After UD's lessons we went to coffee shops where we drank strong Arabian coffee sweetened with honey and listened to Beat authors recite their works. We were bearded and scruffy with long tangled hair, and I was usually shoeless. No one ever doubted our sincerity.

At night there was live jazz at Birdland where luminaries such as Nina Simone, Charlie "Bird" Parker, and John Coltrane played to a small audience of subterranean hipsters. Ours might be the only white faces, but no one seemed to mind, jazz being the one true apotheosis of calm. We arrived stoned and marveled as Coltrane slipped backstage letting his group carry the melodies. He returned cool, aloof, fingering intricate mysteries delivered on a vibrating reed. His notes were gossamer fractals rushing on, receding, shape-shifting improbably, a quaking aurora against the cold black sky. They could settle over you thin as dust or in delicate transparent shapes, ignite your nerves, lull the senses, shatter comfort like fine crystal thrown against stone.

It wasn't so much the music as the silences that separated and pushed apart the notes. That and the dim light swirling in the smoky residue of cigarettes and weed, both riding atop a denser vapor of spilled whiskey, and when it ended and Coltrane disappeared for good behind the curtain there was nothing left to be said. Absolutely nothing.

UD aspired to an elegant squalor. He liked wearing his hair and scraggly beard, his distressed denims and custom sandals. He bought the sandals from a beatnik in the Village who made them out of leather and old tires. You stood on a sheet of paper and the guy drew your foot so that each pair was just you alone right down to the ten toes, themselves individuals. The finished product was a kind of insurance against future hive living.

UD liked driving that Merc with papa ax, his semi-shiny tenor sax riding the back seat nestled beside baby ax, the silver flute, snug inside its tiny casket. He enjoyed walking around rubber-boned and wobble-headed saying, Bop-bidda-debop-*hoo*-debop-boom-*waaa* to music only he could hear, lifting one leg and drumming out the rhythm on his knee. There was the daily practicing of scales in the attic and exercises assigned by his teacher, a recovering jazz musician himself. Once he demonstrated his teacher's flute version of "Summertime" to Cap, who was taking a bath. Uncle D., sitting astride the crapper, had lost himself in the music when Mrs. Keating burst in suspecting an auditory crisis in the walls, whistling squirrels maybe, or something dangerously electrical.

Another attic resident around that time was Sky King, a bearded fried egg of forty or so with flickering hands and distressed eyes magnified behind thick glasses held together with tape. Sky had the disposition of a wounded badger, the body odor of a musk ox, and passed most days sitting mutely on his bunk drawing palsied images of strange beings who appeared to be floating in space. His sentences when they came were cosmic too, drilling you like random electrons spewed from a quantum universe; Scrabble played by the drooling and short-circuited. He lived on disability checks and spent most of his money on art supplies, drugs, and booze. We sometimes gave him beer, for which he never thanked us.

Once when UD was about to leave for his music lesson Sky asked to go along. He seemed happy, UD said later, weathered face reflecting morning sunshine, babbling and flush with disability money. He said, Hoo it's bright here! Damnation! Lookee them treads all wore thin, I think we'll die. . . .

He pointed to an art store in the Village where they sold special brushes. UD dropped him off in thin rain and returned later to find him soaked and raving on a sidewalk spotted black with chewing gum, being photographed by Japanese tourists. Back at the Evelyn House we dried Sky off, cleaned his glasses, set him on his bunk. We gave him beer and his sketchpad and agreed that local color is whatever you imagined it to be, even the shouting stranger.

I got a night job as a dishwasher at the Seashell Club, a beachfront hotel and nightspot that had just opened in Beach Haven. It was packed and all the rage. Dinner was served until late, and my shift ran from seven through midnight, sometimes spilling over into early morning. There were dozens of waitresses, but one was especially striking. She had long brown legs and a fluffy softness that made you want to take her on your lap and stroke her bald. The waitresses walked past the dishwashing station on their way from the dining room to the kitchen, and I started saying hello when I saw her. After a night or two of pretending I was a stack of dishes she stopped to chat.

I really like you, I said.

Hmmm, she answered, I'm not so sure, and she gave a private little smile.

I also like your nice white teeth, I added, trying to appear dentulous.

You don't seem ambitious, she remarked, leaning against the wall in her waitress dress with all that leg showing.

You must be kidding, I said, I'm working my ass off!

Yes, but dirty dishes?

I turned fully around. You want ambition? Why, I'll chew every bit of shoe leather and checkered gabardine right off you and pick my teeth on the bra snaps. You'll be licked clean of perfume and blue eyeliner in no time, even toenail polish. Could take a while, say, all night.

Hmmm, she said again, that's intriguing, but I think I'll hold out for a doctor who shaves and cuts his hair, and she strode away on her legs through the double doors, flashing me a backward toothpaste smile.

You're making a terrible mistake! I yelled, brandishing a greasy steak platter. *I'm a carnivore and eat no vegetable but the cotton panty!*

Our boss was named Chef. At least that's what he told us to call him. Chef was hunkering and black, leaning at you out of some private gloom when he talked. His wife, who could have been his twin sister, was the salad chef. Everyone called her Mrs. Chef, including Chef.

There was lots of pressure on Chef as head of the kitchen to produce those dinners, each a digestible masterpiece, and he lightened the load with bourbon. By ten at night he was emanating a sour odor of stress and barking at everyone in sight. It was nothing for him to grab a stack of heated plates and smash them on the floor, then order the first poor bastard he saw to sweep up the mess. And if a customer sent back a steak because it was too raw or overcooked there was pandemonium. We dishwashers—there were three of us—were lowest in the kitchen pecking order, well below the chefs and waitresses. One of us usually did the sweeping. Boy! he'd yell at us in a striking reversal of the Southern racial pejorative I was used to hearing. You . . . white boy! Get your pale ass over here with a broom!

Mostly everyone worked like dogs, the waitresses coming and going at a half-trot, the chefs shouting and hustling through the smoke of the grill and setting down orders. The dishes piled up, and we put them through the assembly line. The bus boys brought them in plastic tubs. We scraped off the food into garbage cans and loaded everything into dish racks set atop a chain-driven conveyor. The conveyor assembly resembled a miniature carwash, the washing section of it enclosed to keep water from flying everywhere. The dishes and silverware were first conveyed through the washer where they were sprayed with scalding soapy water, then through a rinse of more scalding water. They came out the other end dry and nearly too hot to touch, but your hands got used to it.

Usually one guy scraped and loaded the dish racks, another unloaded and stacked the clean dishes and sorted silver, and the third scrubbed pots and skillets. My partners were Woody, a student at Bucknell who could recite Baudelaire in the French, and a skinny slacker on the bum. This guy wore lots of tattoos in a time when only bikers and jailbirds had them. One night Woody and I turned the water in the dishwasher to cold, held the slacker down on some empty dish racks, and ran him through an accelerated cycle of wash and rinse. After that he worked harder, but Chef gave us hell when he quit laughing.

The dishwashers ate like kings. We convinced the waitresses to slow down as they passed by our station if they were returning wrongly cooked steaks, which Chef would throw in the trash anyway. We scarfed them on the spot, sometimes scooping up a handful of vegetables or mashed potatoes while the waitresses stood there holding the plates, impatient and slightly disgusted. But I really ate well starting the day after Mrs. Chef got wind of Chef fooling around with our one black waitress. She went looking for him with the cleaver she used to lop heads of lettuce in half.

It was early in the evening. Chef was having a few pops at the bar to lubricate his yelling voice so she went there first. Chef must have seen the cleaver and the look in her eye and bolted for the kitchen. I was the first person he found. He said, Mrs. Chef's fixing to cut off my nuts! You got to hide me, boy! I shoved him into the walk-in cooler seconds before Mrs. Chef arrived pissed and patulous and thinking dismemberment. He went to the beach, I told her, and she slammed through the back door and disappeared. I opened the cooler and Chef eased out of the fog.

Lord Jesus it's cold in there, he said, wrapping himself in hands like porterhouses. But what am I supposed to do? When she gets like this she stays pissed for days.

Send her flowers, I offered, and a box of chocolates. The idea was a revelation. I suggested going to the concierge and getting her to do it, considering his inexperience. The next day they were like newlyweds.

That night he pulled me off station. You saved my ass, white boy. You like steaks to take home? Help yourself anytime. So I did, shoveling them out the back door to Cap and UD along with twice-baked potatoes, fresh vegetables, anything that looked tasty.

It got so they said, Shit, filets again?

I'd say, How about Cornish hen?

Cornish hen works, Cap would say.

Yeah, Cornish hen's good, UD would add. Can you get us any beer?

Chef doesn't control the beer.

Damn shame, they said. Does he control the stuffed shrimp?

Eventually I quit the Seashell Club, but Cap got a night job in a pizzeria where the owner taught him to spin dough on his finger. He and Cap, looking breaded and bakerly in white flour, stood at the front window on full display spinning out ten-inch, twelve-inch, fourteen-inch disks of pizza dough while the customers watched and even cheered. Sometimes I went in Joe's car to pick up Cap at the end of his shift. It would be late, one or two in the morning, and we ate a pizza before going back to the rooming house. On certain days that was all I ate.

This must have been my second year on the island because Joe's car was now minus a roof and windshield. Cap and his buddies had driven it from college in Lake Placid to Montreal and rolled it over. There was nothing to be done about the caved-in roof except take it off with a blowtorch. Cap said driving that winter nearly gave him frostbite, never mind the snow inside up to your armpits.

One morning he and I decided to go to Atlantic City and hang out around the boardwalk. We both had a couple of free days and a little spare cash so we borrowed Joe's car. On the way out of Beach Haven we bought a case of beer for the ride. I remember the day as sunny and hot, and the bugs hitting us full in the face at seventy miles an hour stung like pellets from an air rifle. We were drinking at a good pace before the beer on the back seat got warm. As a general category of sin, littering in 1960 wasn't considered the equivalent of homosexual marriage or failure to separate your trash at the curb, as it is today, and we were tossing empties onto the Garden State Parkway through the convenient hole where the roof used to be.

It was also a time before national paranoia over drunk driving, and the state trooper could not have been nicer. You're endangering other drivers, he said, by forcing them to dodge your beer cans. I'd advise you to leave them in the car. Yessir, we said. He checked Cap's driver's license, then he asked, Where's the inspection sticker? In fact, where's the windshield?

We don't have a windshield, Cap replied, but here's the sticker. He reached into the glove box and took out a little piece of glass with the sticker attached. It expired the next day.

The trooper looked at it. You're living right, he said. Now stay out of trouble.

We parked in front of a dive off the boardwalk, went in, and ordered dime drafts. It was about noon. Then it was midnight. The bar was open twenty-four hours. The next morning we were still sitting there. The morning bartender said, You guys still here? Have you eaten? No, we said, but the idea was not a bad one so we ordered burgers with onions and more beer.

One of us, I forget which, looked out the window and recognized a good-looking blonde in a white waitress dress tripping down the sidewalk. I believe it was Cap who saw her first. That's Rosie Rottencrotch, he said. I looked too, and it surely was. Rosie was probably the best-looking girl at West Nottingham Academy our last year there. In fact, she was very, very good looking, but more than a little snooty. Out of spite and a desperate horniness we nicknamed her Rosie Rottencrotch. Now she was walking right toward us, that familiar wiggle in her step.

Drunk and stinking we slid off our stools and ran outside to greet her. She wrinkled her nose and stepped back as if a foul slobbering thing had just humped across her path. Rosie was always gorgeous in a frazzled way, but this day she looked brushed and lingered over.

You guys, she said. I was hoping you died.

We asked what she was doing, which was tossing them off the arm in a restaurant between semesters. She had a fiancé back at school and sneered as she bent her wrist to show us the ring, arm stretched out and already gaining distance. 'Bye, she said, and I hope to never see you again. She never did. That afternoon, still drunk, we drove back to Long Beach Island having seen Atlantic City.

Why is it that observation and insight are decoupled so remotely? Certain images have never gone away: morning light pooling on bare tables, exhaled smoke like moving finger paint across a dirty window. This is what my eyes saw unaccompanied by any prescience or epiphany. Cap's impending alcoholism lay buried along with my own fading availability to either compassion or altruism; that and a shivering dread of ever being responsible for someone else. The hollowness in Cap's eyes, his laughter banked quickly by silence, should have been a warning. I can picture the walls and floor, the patrons hunched over their dimies and hoping—praying—to once again slip away in blackness. Perhaps our heroic visions had once been theirs.

On reflection I see evidence that memory's fragments sustain continuity of the conscious self. Above the rows of bottles I imagine a line taken from Denis Johnson's *Jesus' Son*: Sometimes what I wouldn't give to have us sitting in a bar again at 9:00 a.m. telling lies to one another, far from God.

5

When I first knew Don Hicks he must have been about thirty-five and aging fast, the quiet kind who nurses a beer and a cigarette off in a corner and slides underneath life's radar doing a slow limbo, although without any obvious remnant of misery. He laughed with his mouth closed, probably because of rotten teeth, looking down at the floor and going humph, humph, humph similar to a rhinoceros with a piece of hay stuck in its throat. Hicks cut his old jeans off at the leg and wore them as shorts along with a matching denim shirt that might have been picked out of a trash bin. This attire was completed by a battered felt hat that clung like a desperate bobcat to the back of his head, and sneakers through which the toes protruded. Jock sandals, he called them.

Hicks had training in marine mechanics, which provided ready employment and good pay in any coastal town, but he preferred life on the bum, sleeping in his car and working only when necessary. Summers he camped on the Jersey shore, winters in Ft.

Lauderdale. Stashed in the cavernous trunk of his beat Pontiac was everything he owned: tools, spare clothes, scuba gear, a razor and shaving soap, and a shoebox containing correspondence and employment records, the whole of it fingerprinted in black grease.

His singular interest was diving on shipwrecks and rummaging around for things of value that could later be sold. Sometimes we went diving together using his equipment, although most of what we found was useless: twisted cables, heavy engine parts sculpted by barnacles and bacterial slime, rusty bolts, pieces of boiler plate. . . . Once we found some copper spikes that Hicks cherished too much to sell, so he kept them.

Nobody we knew was certified to dive. You learned by doing it and later listening to someone who was truly ignorant and a confirmed liar tell stories of the near bends and close encounters with sharks. Basically you opened the air valve, strapped the apparatus to your back, and jumped overboard. An air gauge was an unnecessary accoutrement; when your air ran out it was time to surface.

Hicks and I were pounding down dimies in Buckalew's late one stormy night at the end of May 1961, the ashtray before us overflowing, elbows awash in pooling condensation. The place seemed almost cozy inside its walls of tormented wood patched over with stuffed fish slain in distant eras and photographs of the long dead. Until the rooming houses opened rented beds were scarce. I'd arrived by bus a couple of days before and run into Hicks drinking coffee at the counter of Kapler's Drugstore. As a result of this good fortune I was flopping on the front seat of his car while he slept in the back. The bar was nearly deserted, a few beery regulars holding forth under lights that had begun to flicker ominously.

The door opened letting in a blast of fresh air followed by a regular patron wearing oilskins who announced that a yacht had foundered on the sandbar offshore, evidently with no one aboard. Where? someone asked. Right at the end of the street, the newcomer said.

Hicks lit a smoke. You know about salvage law? he asked me.

No, I answered.

Well, he said, whoever gets to a stranded vessel first and establishes a permanent presence holds the salvage rights to her. It's universal maritime law.

No shit, I said.

Maybe we should salvage this one, Hicks said, you and me. There's got to be a helluva lot of valuable stuff on board.

Tom the bartender interrupted. Yeah, right, how're you going to get out there? You got a boat? We're in a major goddamn nor'easter.

We'll swim out, Hicks answered. We'll sit on her until the storm breaks, at which point she'll be ours. It was a stupid idea, which Tom let us know by shaking his head and waddling down the bar to hear someone else's bullshit, not that our end of it was lacking.

You want sea laws? I'll tell you sea laws, said Edgar. He leaned past me to look at Hicks. Edgar was rheumy of eye and no stranger to halitosis. His Social Security check went mostly for rent and dimies and enough cigarettes to last the month. Edgar obtained his clothes, including shoes and used eyeglasses, by bumming rides to the Salvation Army over on the mainland. He claimed it was cheaper than the Laundromat.

You don't know jack-shit about the law, Edgar, chimed in Freddy Dahl, resident philosopher and clam digger. Maritime law is quite complicated, he continued, his voice becoming stentorian, and certainly beyond someone who never studied anything more profound than his own bellybutton. Freddy belched loudly. He was loaded and trying gamely to mount his soapbox.

Edgar turned on him. What makes you so fucking smart? he snarled. Did you go to college? Are you a lawyer? I don't think so. He took a sip from this glass that might have been dangerously aggressive unless you knew him.

Freddy, using height to advantage, peered over Edgar's head at Hicks and me. He said, as if in Edgar's absence, Edgar doesn't adum . . . doesn't, uh, adumbrate the shallowness of his knowledge. Please forgive him, he added, as if we were visiting dignitaries.

Goddammit, Freddy, I ain't the dumbass you think I am, said Edgar. When I was working the bay we rescued lots of boats and towed them to shore, but we didn't own none of them. Sometimes there was people on them, sometimes not. Once we towed in a bunch of naked men and women all drunk and acting stupid. Guess they was having a party and throwed their clothes overboard.

Naked women? It was an old guy on the other side of Freddy. He tried seeing over and around Freddy but was too short, so he got down off his stool and came and stood like a stooped heron behind Edgar. He was breathing hard. Did you see their pussies?

Of course I did, you fool. And one, she had a shaved pussy, only one I ever seen in my life.

A shaved pussy, the old-timer repeated. He said it thoughtfully, not recalling if the notion repulsed or excited him. What did you do with them?

What did I do with what? asked Edgar, who had spun around on his stool.

With them naked women.

Julius, for chrissakes what do you think we done? We give them blankets to cover up their nakedness.

And a hot toddy, Freddy added. Etiquette, if not maritime law, demands that victims of sea tragedies be given hot liquids to prevent hypothermia, preferably with rum.

It was August, Freddy, Edgar said, and hot enough to fry an egg on your forehead. But I seen more pussy that day than I ever seen before or since, and it all looked good.

The old-timer, Julius, was speechless. He stood between Edgar and Freddy staring at nothing. Wished I'd of been there, he mumbled.

Well, we have work to do, Hicks said. We downed our beers and stepped outside into vicious curtains of cold rain, stumbling east to where illumination from the streetlights paled to blackness. The night felt thick enough to wear across your shoulders like a wet dog. We were dressed in sunny-weather shorts and shirts and drunk past the point of walking properly even in the sunshine. No clothes to leave behind! I yelled at Hicks.

No one to claim the body! he yelled back, which was true.

Hicks lived without those simple memories of a sandbox and toy truck underneath the leafy maple. It was just himself, a fading series of gray silhouettes shocked faceless by any thought of heritage and love. In my company he once recalled an unnamed cancer victim, perhaps his mother, and someone else who succumbed in a vague year to irregularities of the heart or pancreas. It was sufficient to invent genealogies during moments of sodden fellowship, fascinating and repelling those who were strangers to him: an uncle with a secret lust for the rectums of men, a child-molesting cousin, lazy-eyed aunts who chanted unchristian languages while burying crosses by moonlight, and Hicks in his formless self, hobo and drunk, invisible inside his own rousing dignity.

Surf noise exploded as we approached the beach, the raindrops seeming to crawl out from a nest of countless stinging things. I decided to puke before swallowing any of the sea that sprang at us in jagged white walls, grabbing our legs and sucking the sand out from under us. The yacht, which appeared momentarily in lightning flashes, was stretched across the sandbar like a beached whale a hundred yards out. We dived under a wave and rode the backwash into deeper water. It occurred to us independently that turning back was impossible. To ride that surf shoreward in the dark would be suicidal, reducing the choices to get there and climb aboard or drown.

The swells lifted us high enough to periodically glimpse the boat through lightning flashes and keep us stroking in its general direction, although we quickly lost sight of each other. Even sober it would have been a harrowing swim, and I arrived to find Hicks clambering up the keel. The yacht was ketch-rigged and lay on its starboard side, bow pointed north. The masts were broken but still intact and along with the keel had dug into the shallow bottom. In combination they served as projecting anchors and were holding the vessel in place.

From my vantage point the boat looked huge and dark, smooth as a bathtub and devoid of any handholds. Waves breaking over the bar kept pushing me back. Just lifting my head to breathe became a struggle. Even worse, there was no visibility at all, nothing that stood out against the blackness until a lightning flash illuminated several loose lines and a large section of flapping canvas, probably a spare sail broken loose. Unbelievably, there was also a rope ladder whipping back and forth. Hicks grabbed it then turned and shouted something inaudible before pulling himself up. I followed.

Climbing that ladder was a lucid dream happening to someone else. I felt the transparent sensation experienced by survivors of armed conflict or a traffic accident, that slowing of time when the conscious self turns passive witness and the phenomenal world seems unreal. The very act of it was so foreign I laughed out loud. Forcing myself to concentrate induced hyperawareness, and I was conscious of breathing, grasping the rope, moving my legs and torso. Just like oriental meditation, I thought, drunken meditation and entirely tactile: the slippery hull, the wind and water, my wasted mind offering up reasons why I should be someplace else that was motionless and dry. The ladder bounced violently back and forth along the hull, macerating some fingers each time it landed.

Eventually I reached the highest point where the vessel's beam was widest, but staying there was like balancing on the edge of a seawall. Waves driven from windward came straight on, riding up the tilted deck and breaking hard, forcing me to grip the rails and lie flat. There was no sign of Hicks. I presumed he was holding on somewhere behind me near the bow, but this could only be confirmed by turning around to look. I waited for a lull in the waves, but their continuous onslaught kept me hunkered down. If Hicks had fallen off the boat then surely he was dead.

I was shaking violently from hypothermia and wondered how much strength remained in my hands. Better to die drunk than sober, I thought, but somehow the idea of being right there was thrilling and the notion of actually dying seemed a joke. In the place of cold and fear was a rush of warmth and exuberance. I felt immediate and alive. A searchlight appeared suddenly and a voice through a bullhorn said, *Hey numbnuts!*

Having noticed Hicks' car still parked at the curb, Tom Buckalew had called the Coast Guard after we left his bar. He told them that two ignorant drunks had just wandered into the storm and were planning to swim out and salvage a yacht off the beach. A coastie we knew as Big Walt, based at the Holgate station, was at the helm and standing off to westward. The Coast Guard tower was located directly on the beach I guarded, and the coasties often swam there and trolled for girls. I knew them all. Big Walt ordered us to let go and drop into the water, saying his guys would pick us up downwind.

I heard about your "salvage" operation, Big Walt said after we were aboard and wallowing back to the station. We decided you were already dead but figured it was right to go check anyway. You need to quit swimming in nor'easters and also smarten up. The setting down of your wet asses atop a vessel don't make for salvage rights. And speaking of which, where the hell are your clothes? Jesus, you're buck naked. What fucking morons. You guys owe me some beers.

Cap arrived on the island shortly after this happened and suggested we get an apartment together, so we rented a dumpy three-room place in Beach Haven on the second floor of a house. It was unfurnished, but we figured to sleep on the floor temporarily and worry about furnishings later.

We bought a frozen chicken and a case of beer and celebrated the first night by eating in. There were no dishes and no silverware so we unwrapped the chicken and set it on one of the trays in the oven. Cap, who was attending hotel management college, knew something about cooking and adjusted the settings. After the first six-pack he went to check and found that the oven had been disconnected. Who cares? we agreed. Barley and hops are food. Quite a bit later we wondered if maybe the oven was hooked up after all and checked again. It was still dead, but the chicken had thawed a little except for the inside, and we ate it raw. A couple of days later some friends came over for a party. The following morning the landlord, who lived downstairs, evicted us.

With the rooming houses still closed our only option was camping on the beach. Cap and I were too broke to rent another place and someone else was now sleeping on the front seat of Hicks' car. Even so, Hicks had room for only one guest. The township had set out the two-man lifeboats in preparation for opening the beaches. They were wooden double-enders, heavy and beamy, and lay upside down in the sand above maximum high tide. We thumbed a ride the three miles or so to Holgate, placed two boats side by side, and moved in underneath. It was pleasant going to sleep with rain beating on the upturned hull.

Holgate comprised the south end of Long Beach Island where Bay Avenue stopped. No roads extended beyond this point. On the west side of the street was Fritz's Liquors, a low shingled building painted dull green and owned by Fritz and his wife Mary. From Bay Avenue west to Barnegat Bay were streets of inexpensive houses and a trailer park. Across Bay Avenue on the ocean side was a pair of large public beaches bisected by a stone jetty. At the base of the jetty was the steel Coast Guard tower painted gray and topped by an observation room where two coasties were always on duty. A row of about six beach houses squatted on pilings among the north beach dunes. Past them was the large abandoned bath house sagging in disrepair, the double doors to its cubicles parted like careless thighs. North of the bath house came two miles of emptiness, then more beach houses and the town of Beach Haven. I was usually stationed at the south beach, which was contiguous with the northern end of a federal bird sanctuary that encompassed the last three miles of the island. The south beach was the larger and ordinarily had more people who needed saving, in part because of a frequent rip current along that side of the jetty during rough weather.

Holgate had two food concessions, a tiny stand near the street and a more extensive operation with a deck and some chairs overlooking the north beach. Both were still locked tight in May. The first of these was operated by a cranky old woman and her middle-aged son. They sold hotdogs, burgers, potato chips, and soft drinks. The old lady could add a column of numbers faster than anyone I've seen before or since. She would run her pencil down its length, mentally compute the tax, and spit out the total in a couple of seconds. Many people didn't believe her and laboriously added the numbers themselves, but she was never wrong.

The other food service was operated by a married couple, Dick and Gladys. Dick was much older, skinny with a gray flattop. He mostly sat around reading the paper and smoking, although when something needed fixing he was right there. Gladys had beautiful violet eyes and a permanent smile. The guards ate at one place or the other when there was cash to spare, which was seldom.

Food was the main problem of camping on the beach before anything opened, and partly for this reason I came every summer equipped with a pole spear, mask, snorkel, and flippers. Fat tautogs and striped bass hung around the jetty. On our first day of camping I swam out to the end and speared a couple of tautogs, and Cap and I cooked them over a driftwood fire. I remember us bitching because there was no salt or pepper and nothing in which to cook the fish. The next day we thumbed back to Beach Haven and picked up some spices, aluminum foil, and potatoes, and subsequent dinners were much tastier.

Seabirds—varied quizzical creatures—were present in abundance, standing around on the sand looking confident and prosperous. The sanctuary was right next door, and the birds were tame enough to approach. Hungry people do strange things, and after several days we needed a change from fish. The literature is filled with tales of starving explorers who ate their sled dogs, then their boots, and finally each other. The memory of that failed chicken dinner haunted us. Using leftover fish heads as bait we lured a great black-backed gull to within reach and wrung its neck. A great black-backed is big and plump, nearly the equal of a small roasting chicken. We plucked this one, cleaned out the guts, washed the carcass in seawater, and cooked it on a makeshift spit. It tasted like fishy mud. For the remaining days until the Evelyn House opened we stuck to seafood.

One afternoon we went across the street and knocked on the door of Fritz's Liquors. No one answered, although a sign said it was open. I knew that Fritz and Mary had an apartment in back so we went around to check, but no one answered the back door either. Fritz and I had become friends ever since I allowed him to walk his dog on the beach after public hours. It was against a township ordinance, but he and Mary were nice people who lived on the island all year, and I figured they deserved special treatment.

We returned to the beach, stepping over the rise from the parking lot, and there stood Fritz in a raincoat, wizened and wispy-haired, eyesight grown dim in the distance. He had white spittle at the corners of his mouth. When he recognized me he smiled sadly. Something didn't feel right, and neither of us reached out a hand to shake the other's.

He said simply, She's gone, you know. Mary had a stroke. Fuck it, he said, and shrugged. He turned and waved his hand as if saying goodbye to the world. Now my dog is crippled like me, he said. His back was to us, and we could barely hear him. I can get a new dog but not a new Mary. Fritz the German immigrant, Mary the Jersey girl, together fifty years or more, now Fritz alone. He and the dog limped away slowly. He waved his hand in a come-along motion without turning and said, Over at the store, a drink, you and me and your friend.

In the store Fritz pulled a quart bottle of bourbon off a shelf, broke the seal, and poured us each a healthy measure in paper cups. Cap and I stood on the customer side of the counter, Fritz on the business side. Then we had several more until the bottle was empty.

Tears formed in Fritz's eyes. I hate the nights, he said. I mentioned we needed beer. Take it and pay me later, he said. I know you ain't got money yet. We extracted a case from the cooler and thanked Fritz and asked if he wanted us to visit him later, but he was staring out the window.

The rest of the summer I never saw Fritz sober, whether behind the counter or walking his dog. He smiled and said hello, but any interaction, even this minimal amount, seemed forced and tired. He looked smaller than I remembered him before, bent over and sinking into the earth as if physically pressed beneath a heavy sadness. The drunkenness was subtle, but I knew Fritz and understood his motive: inhabiting an alcoholic stupor deadened pain, shortened the days, attenuated the memories that made him crazy.

I offered to volunteer at the store during evenings, but he waved me away. He had to do it himself, he said, which I assumed meant survive. Some afternoons after the beach closed I went over and we had a drink together. I stood silently on the customer side of the counter looking down at my paper cup and sloshing the brown bourbon around while he stared out the window. That was the nature of our friendship, but I figured the time and the pain were his, and whatever he wanted to do or say was alright. Fritz died that winter. His liver failed, some said, but surely it had been his heart.

The afternoon was cold and spitting rain with a gray sea slopping against the jetty, but we were out of fish. Reluctantly I stripped to skivvies, grabbed the gear, and swam out through the surf. The tide was low, the water depth at the end of the jetty about eight feet and turbid. Stripers, which fade to the color of nickel, were especially difficult to see in late afternoon against the background light. I speared two tautogs instead of looking further, sliding the first up the length of the spear to hold it in place. Tautogs were predictable, always near the rocks.

Back on the beach I stood in the rain for a time to wash away the salt, then dried off on my clothes before putting them back on. We cleaned the fish and sloshed the fillets in the surf.

Eventually the rain stopped, allowing a fire to be started with dry driftwood stored underneath the boats. Once that got going we added wet wood a little at a time until there were hot ashes enough to take potatoes and fish wrapped in aluminum foil. A cold fog crept up in darkness out of the sea. We leaned back, church-keyed two cold ones, lit cigarettes, and agreed that life could hardly get better.

*I*n 1959, my first year at Beach Haven, the township paid its lifeguards thirty-five dollars a week to start, and every year you came back the pay increased by five dollars. We worked six days from ten until six with a half-hour break for lunch. After Social Security's bite and eight dollars going to rent, little remained for food, drink, and cigarettes. Being broke was the normal state. To save money most of us talked up the beach regulars, ordinarily young mothers with kids, convincing them to bring us lunch occasionally, or at least a sandwich.

The morning routine was to drag the lifeguard stands down close to the surf and get the "cans" out of the storeroom where Dick and Gladys let us keep them. Cans were hexagonal floating blocks of hard Styrofoam painted red, their edges ringed with rope handles. When someone needed saving you grabbed a can, ran into the surf, swam to the victim, and told him to hang on. Then you swam back doing the sidestroke and pulling the can. If the victim was too weak you draped him over the can, pinning him between the can and yourself, and kicked in. None of this was easy because most "runs," or life-saving episodes, occurred in rough surf or rip currents, and there could be several in a day. Also, we were usually hung over or still drunk if the party had lasted all night.

The guards at Holgate got together and made several improvements designed to relieve physical exertion. Bill Beron was a guard then. Beron, who always needed a shave and had a crooked Italian stogie stuck in his face, was a carpenter during the winter and good with tools. There was UD, who was pretty much useless where real work was called for, and a guy nicknamed Chang who resembled an oriental if you had never seen one before, but he was just your overweight Caucasian boy with squinty eyes.

Two wooden telephone cable reels had washed up one night during a storm. With Dick's tools we drilled holes in the frame underneath the seats of the stands and strung a reel under each using a length of pipe so the reels could spin freely. Dick devised crank handles on the ends of the pipes and welded them on. We tied two hundred feet of rope to each reel and the other ends to cans, and we now had devices for "reeling in" victims. Lifesaving became similar to fishing except that one guard still had to swim out with the can attached to the rope.

After several runs it became apparent that reeling was nearly as tiring as swimming for the guard left on the beach. At his station farther up the island Cap had devised a scheme for deputizing kids to watch the water when crowds were small and conditions calm, allowing the occasional nap. We deputized some of the bigger kids at Holgate, most of whom were there for the summer, and trained them to crank the handles, one on each side. We also discovered that towing the can out became much easier if you wore flippers. Lifesaving suddenly got simpler and less likely to induce morning vomiting, which paradoxically seemed to erode public confidence.

More than one beach regular stopped by and asked, Are you guys okay? I mean, you seem less screwed up than usual.

Just gaining on technology, sir, nothing to be alarmed about, but your daughter looks about twelve, and I'd keep an eye on her. Can't trust those horny guards over on the north beach.

Really? That's what they said about you.

Art Jocker, captain of the guards, even came down to see what we were doing, rumor of advancements in lifesaving technology having spread all the way to the town hall. Jocker was a middle-aged high school football coach, large and intimidating with steely blue eyes. He never talked much, preferring to stand in silence with arms crossed Bear Bryant fashion, baseball cap pulled down over the brows, chewing his gum slowly like a ruminating steer. That day he parked the Jeep with "Captain" painted on its doors and came over to the stand where I sat with another guard. He stood beside us looking out at the water. No one spoke. After a minute or two he turned and left.

*W*e avoided the lifeboats except for required practice runs once a week. In fact we never used a lifeboat to save a person, at least that I can recall. The usual team of two guys could barely push one of these tubs into the surf, and then you had to row in tandem with your back to the victim hoping you weren't running him over or stroking in the wrong direction. In heavy surf they were a liability.

Every year in midsummer the township participated in the lifeguard relays where we competed against Beach Haven and Surf City guards in timed swims to a victim while towing a can, the parallel shore swim, the lifeboat race, and other events invented by otherwise unemployable football coaches. The year the relays were hosted by Holgate, Beales and Beron were supposed to row for us, except that Beales, our lieutenant, was on hands and knees that morning puking up the previous night's party. The rest of us were also experiencing nausea and major disorientation, having attended the same party. We disqualified ourselves from competition, instead recruiting Big Walt and another coastie who were off duty and sunbathing near the tower with some girls. We promised them a case of beer for win, place, or show. Big Walt subsequently won the parallel beach swim, and he and his buddy were second in rowing. It wasn't until the next day that Jocker came down and reamed us for substituting ringers and making him look bad in front of the other captains.

Sometimes a busload of inner-city blacks from Philly would drive down Bay Avenue looking for a beach to picnic and swim for the day. Township guards were encouraged to turn them away, saying that parking buses there was illegal or finding another excuse. Eventually they might arrive at Holgate—literally the end of the road—where we encouraged them to stay. Relieved and happy they shoveled food at us until we were stuffed: fried chicken, potato salad, greens, homemade pudding, iced tea. And what they forgot they bought from the old lady or Gladys. Nobody suffered.

Once they brought us a huge watermelon, icy cold. This melon is special, they said, laughing. The night before they had cut cores from it, filled the holes with vodka, reinserted the plugs of rind, and stuck it in a refrigerator. It was a 90-proof watermelon. I got drunk eating slices in the hot sun and fell off the stand to simultaneous applause from the black donors and white regulars from the trailer park. This incident was reported to Jocker, who told Beales to fire me. Jocker had never approved of my beard and unkempt hair. Basically I was a disgrace to the swimsuit. Drinking on the beach, he reportedly said, was the last straw, although as I pointed out to a sympathetic Beales, technically it was eating on the beach, which was not against the rules.

I took a night job washing dishes at a diner. The clientele consisted mostly of shuffling alcoholics and bored hoodlums with nowhere else to go. The night cook was a drunk himself and somewhat lacking in teeth. He never bothered asking my name, and I had no interest in knowing his. We worked side by side without speaking, often for an hour or two, then it was, I need that skillet clean, and I would say okay or nothing at all.

June beetles, shiny and brown as new penny loafers, entered through the open door crazed and seeking light. Many tumbled into the deep-fat fryer to be cooked and served along with French fries and onion rings and the occasional tiptoeing roach that had lost its footing in the grease. I never heard a complaint, and probably no one noticed. After the place closed at midnight I threw disinfectant on the floor and left it there for the daytime dishwasher to mop up.

A couple of weeks passed. I was lying on my cot reading one morning when there was a hefty laboring noise from the stairs. I looked up and saw Jocker's capped head. Christ, he muttered while trying to catch his breath, you guys live like pigs. Not even a damn phone so I could call. These might have been his longest spoken sentences ever, until the next when he continued, I don't understand it, why this would happen, I mean, why they would want you, but the Holgate residents petitioned the township to get you reinstated. I just don't understand, but what the hell, you can start back working your beach tomorrow if you want. The stairs and all that talking must have been exhausting because he turned and left without waiting for an answer. So the next day I went back.

Beales stood up on the stand and stretched. Good morning, asshole, he said. When Jocker fired you he made me rotate over, and I'm tired of sitting on this fucking chair all day. He yawned. If any good-looking women stop by, get their names and numbers for me.

Fat chance of that, I said.

UD's music teacher introduced him to an artsy New York crowd, and he was hanging around its fringes sucking up the occasional crumb. He said Ida Puente liked riding behind him on his motor scooter, snuggling up close and pressing her titties into his back. This was when her husband Tito was playing at the Palladium in Manhattan. UD told us Tito was queer and didn't care what Ida was doing. The rest of us attic denizens said we didn't care either, which hurt UD's feelings, sensitive as he was.

There were painters, musicians, even dress designers in this crowd. UD had extolled the benefits of Long Beach Island, and some of them started coming down to Beach Haven on weekends as a break from the city. They loved the sun and surf, the strange locals, and the casual attitude. It was, they said, Greenwich Village at the beach. Among them were a painter named Artie and his friend Jack, a dress designer.

When they first got down they sought out UD, their only contact from New York, and he arranged rooms with Mrs. Keating at the Evelyn House. After having registered, UD brought them up to the attic to meet everyone. Jack held out his hand with the wrist bent like a French lady to all of us in turn, saying demurely, Call me Camille. As Cap told me later, he didn't know whether to kiss the fucking thing or shake it.

We said they could be our token queers and hang out with us, which they did, telling us that we could be their token bohemians and wasn't it a crying shame we were straight. Artie usually passed unnoticed in a male crowd except when he drank too much and made suggestive remarks or groped the testicles of an unsuspecting yachtsman, but Jack was a dedicated swish who loved coming up the attic stairs wearing lipstick and eye shadow, a woman's beach hat, and his pink Speedo. It helped none that his spare little body was covered all over with a pelt of curly black hair. We laughed tears as he strutted like a runway model up and down the narrow space between our bunks, holding his hat in place with one hand, tilting back his head to give us saucy looks, and wiggling his butt.

Soon they all started showing up at Holgate, and weekends at the south beach were a raucous gathering of Philly street blacks, New York City queers, Jersey station-wagon suburbia, and Holgate trailer trash. One regular, a millionaire advertising executive, typically ended each day passed out in his folding chair, a lumpy brown coprolite oozing bourbon and suntan lotion. After closing I usually lugged him over to his beachfront house or fetched his wife to help, but in this emerging camaraderie there were always offers of assistance.

This guy knew all there was about preying on the unsuspecting public, and he spoke about it with a breathy unctuousness of the true believer. Everything he owned, he said, had been acquired based on judicial use of language and the obliging ignorance of those who read or listened to it. His chair one day was up against the lifeguard stand, and I was ground-level leaning next to it squeezing my butt cheeks together trying to pinch one off. He said that certain words are smooth and wholesome, one being "smooth," another "wholesome," and you want to get these placed strategically in the ad if the product is, say, a manufactured food like cereal.

I squeezed harder. Words the opposite of wholesome must be addressed—no attacked—in dramatic fashion, he continued. Consider a floor cleanser. You don't want it to merely remove dirt, but fight it, erase it, kill it, metaphorically of course, aggressively, the implication being this is a war you can win if you buy our product. Then there's the marketing target—men, women, kids, families—and you approach all these except the men using such words as "soft" and "sweet" and "healthy" and "fun." For guys you substitute "hard" and "tough" and "durable." Get the idea? he asked, mixing us both another highball from the cooler. Hell, it's easy, he said, because your basic consumer is dumber than a lampshade. Just then I released the sphincter and let it go, a fart born to rip fabric. I hadn't meant to, but there it went. The guy didn't even look up. Couldn't have expressed it better, he said.

*F*riendships on the south beach spilled across false boundaries of status and race. People threw balls around, picnicked together, shared recipes and stories and photographs, argued politics and sports, watched someone else's kids, took turns making trips across the street to Fritz's Liquors, and sometimes nearly drowned. In the new egalitarianism people jostled to crank the handles and reel us in, cheering victim and guard as we lurched out of the surf and inundating us with food and drink. Usually our runs were for Philly people, who had never learned to swim. As a resident of the inner city explained to Beron and me, Most of the brothers is sinkers.

UD, retired on unemployment, would be there too lying regally on a blanket and gazing outward in the ricocheted sun, a full disturbance of the ecosystem, while two striking blondes we dated rubbed baby oil on his skin. He gloried in the day, a beat Marlon Brando freshly hatched and living every succulent moment at the edge of his shell. Even then it was late. We had already passed through without a mark, charged ions riding outward on the solar wind. Sand retains no memory, and by morning our footprints would be gone. In the end so would we. UD, innocent, all of us innocent, believed this moment was meant for us alone, and no one ever thought it could end.

Sometimes when the sea breeze quit a torpor swept over us. People had talked themselves hoarse and lay exhausted as if dissolving inwardly. Even the surf looked jaded, crawling limply toward the beach before flopping over in a thin white line. On these days of stale silences Camille might suddenly shout, Hey UD, you could have me instead of those skanky bitches!

The two blondes would laugh and jump up and strut their identical green bikinis, weaving single file among the towels and blankets and saying in their best Marilyn Monroe imitations, Why should he when he can have us?

And Camille would say, This is why, sweeties, and start a strut of his own holding the brim of his big floppy hat and tossing random sultry glances at dark hipsters and dour pineys, embarrassed young fathers and stoned bohemians, lips an artful pink hole of Revlon pressing air kisses. Then the beach went wild, everyone wallowing in a false hope that this was the universe where we would always roll like exalted sea gods in the night, scrabbling after a phosphorescent hunger and calling in each other's glow: Here! Now! Forever!

6

*U*ncle Dirty labored all day and into the night writing a poem, cot bobbing on wavelets of crumpled paper; his tortured sighs were the wind. He murdered a mosquito, looked in astonishment at his pencil, lay back and sought inspiration from the cobwebs overhead. A knee drew up as he scratched his balls and explained to us how the muse has delicate ears. Thereafter the fan blades clattered through silence interrupted once by muttered envy of Coleridge's opium dreams. If only. . . . *I need dope!* he shouted, and someone passed a joint.

The rest of us were nothing if not supporters of the arts. Scarcely breathing, Cap, Artie, and I delivered beer and whispered encouragement while Roy sat nearby sipping rum from a bottle and stifling his screams. Hicks lit cigarettes for the straining poet and emptied his ashtray. Camille crept off to a corner to freshen his lipstick under better light, and even Sky was mute with awe, body odor standing attentively like a thing apart.

Heavy perspiring in pursuit of the perfect word, the measured meter. Soft moans almost sensuous. An anguished palm held against the forehead where delicacy and beauty conspire to escape. Onward trudged the bard, groaning through pangs of creation, impaling banality, repelling the mundane phrase. Finished at last he stood on his cot: cherished colleagues and cocksuckers, mendicants and mudpackers, I now read you my poem:

> Never flips to breeze my ass
> while ginzels through the snitchel pass,
> But nibbles while the pecker please
> rank wizzle-trots upon the knees.
>
> And nevermore the floor shall whore
> upon her wimps dost floppest,
> But dribbles out the umscal brips
> from comes from last we didst.

UD and literal truth had long since parted company even then, but in Key West he recounted to Cap and me scenes from the sixties that placed him in orbit with the weird and famous. He claimed to have shot a pistol at floating cans in a creek with Abbie Hoffman, nearly concussing themselves deaf. There was the recounting of times when he dropped acid with Timothy Leary, smoked reefer with Baba Ram Dass, rapped with Aldous Huxley about the value of entraining LSD into New York City's water supply.

He was living in the East Village keeping company with a growing heroin addiction. That and a lack of willpower eventually conquered the few remnants of optimism. He was now too busy getting high to practice music, and when other junkies stole his sax and flute any hope of self-realization vanished. He became an artisan instead.

The choice had been wrong anyway. Creeping over the jazz scene like a fungus came the distant anorgasmic vibrato of Joan Baez and Bob Dylan's sophomoric rhymes. The zeitgeist of the sixties soon focused on art as performance instead of purity, devolving into selfishness and a general ignorant rage: those still averse to selling out saw no conflict with ripping off friends or collecting unemployment. When the antiwar movement heated up UD joined those riotous throngs and hustled young wannabe nooky. All that posturing came to nothing when American forces exited Saigon, and then you saw former protestors with graying ponytails and no social agenda still bumming smokes in Tompkins Square Park. Nothing undermines revolution like success.

By the time Cap and I found UD dying in Staunton, Virginia, in the autumn of 2006 he was anomic and dragging the baggage of a spiritual poverty that slid over into near bereavement. A few pieces remained from his glass-blowing days, and we bought them so he could make the rent and buy dope and whiskey. Medicare was paying medical bills and Social Security not covering the rest. The landlady had his weight; friends were checking in and bringing groceries. Events were not cohesive. Once before the phone company shut down his line he sent us an e-mail that said,

> Capt. Russ and Doc. I oftenwanted to be emeperor. Then I reaolzed it was an alcoholic fantacy. Will you help me write my memuars? Gof domg this fucjung brike keybuard!!!!!!!!!!!!!!!! Art sucks. UD

Near the end he was in a traffic accident at a mall. A woman in a van crashed into his tattered Bronco and broke his hip. I talked to him after he got home from the hospital. Cap and I sent money so he could pay the phone bill and revitalize his stash.

That fucking bitch, she crashed right into me! he ranted.

Were you stoned? I asked.

Of course! he replied. Drunk too, but the cops said it was her fault. I'm going to sue her. Shit, I can't even walk.

You in a cast?

Naw, they nailed me together with pins. Hey, thanks for the bread, man, you and Cap have really helped out. It's been a pleasure to know you both, a true pleasure. Cowboys forever, right? Am I a drag, being sick and all? I could hear his breath like air escaping through a decrepit valve.

Wart on the ass of progress, I said.

Then he said, The cancer's bad, very bad, but know what? I don't give a fuck anymore.

That was the last coherent thing he told me. In July one of his Staunton buddies, Craig Holt, telephoned to tell me UD had slipped away into morphine dreams. It was over.

What's UD been like these last years? I asked Craig.

Awful. You couldn't possibly know unless you lived in Staunton. He was incredibly demanding, filled up your days if you weren't careful just to drive him here and there: grocery store, liquor store, post office . . . a real pain in the ass. His Bronco hardly ever ran. If you balked he gave you this hangdog look. If you flat told him you didn't have time to be a chauffeur *right then* or had personal errands to run or maybe a minor family emergency he'd look away and say stuff like, Okay, man, I'm down on my luck, you know? I mean, I thought we were friends but I understand, I understand . . . you've got your own thing. And then of course I'd cave and run him all over town and afterward he'd get out and walk away without saying thanks. My wife is a nurse at the hospital. She did everything possible for him whenever he checked in, and what did *he* do? He complained like it was a hotel with poor service. This last episode with the broken hip? They also put him through a week of mandatory detox. Think the hospital staff enjoyed that?

UD told me he was suing the woman who ran her car into his and broke his hip, I said.

UD didn't have a car then, Craig said. I'd already taken away his keys and we'd given the Bronco to his brother when he came down from Jersey. UD wasn't hit by anyone, he fell in the parking lot. I was there. I called the ambulance.

UD was one of those few you meet who stick in the mind, always fresh and vivid, sensitive as sunburned skin. I recalled him describing to Cap and me in Key West how he wanted to blink out while stoned and hoped someone would hold a doobie to his lips. Why is it, he asked, that when we look around for a mountain to die on the only thing in sight is a pile of dirty laundry? Why can't romance be manufactured, at least temporarily? This old friend Cap and I saw had acquired Kerouac's beatific aura. It gathered about him mistlike until he seemed ennobled and almost saintly. Once as we walked into town with UD staggering along behind out of earshot, Cap said, UD is probably the coolest guy in the world. It was hard to disagree. Time and illness had taken him to a state beyond cool where such normal human failings as perfidy and envy have been set aside. Nothing mattered any longer. He lived in ambivalence: a shrug, a vaguely upturned palm, a raised eyebrow—any of these gestures could stand in for a violent opinion. He passed through the hours dazed, serene, gazing out with the numinous clarity of a gaunt and tipsy angel.

He caught up to us. Know what? You guys have great memories. My own suck. In the traffic noise we could barely hear his words hissed out through the throat blood and cigarette smoke. He told us his motto, which is to live and forgive unless you're a stinking Bush-loving Republican loud-mouthed woman-beating hypocritical evangelistic yuppie money-grubbing scumbag who doesn't munch down on pussy.

Hear, hear, we said. That use of breath had been costly. With rough sympathy we steadied him, one on each thin arm, seeking to pirouette away from extinction. A cancerous prostate had shown me the void and Cap, nonplussed after recent lung cancer surgery, had surely glimpsed it too. We paused so Cap could light a fresh butt, his face a laughing prophecy of doom. Linked like that we lurched to the next cross street, unsteady revenants in triumphant decline.

UD's agony obviated any reprising of pain on my part or Cap's, assuming such experiences could be possible. He was drifting away from us even as we held him, disappearing into the ether a molecule at a time. Little remained now except ambulating bones and an unspoken bequest, the static image of some future sorrow even as his own faded. I was stoned but not mellow, here instead of there, and sensing a need to shout how I'd looked underneath every rock in my path for sixty-five years and found nothing useful. I wanted to announce how everyone simply dies and oxidizes, but my companions already knew. There can be no deaths that are holy or unselfish or brave or transient, not when death is unconditional. If you burn to believe in an afterlife, then pray for the perpetuation and recombination of matter. Believe in recycling. I glanced at UD in the twilight and saw only vapor. Isn't God funny? I thought. Such a relentless chemist.

It was Yeats who claimed only sex and death are of interest to serious minds. I know one thing, one certain fact: life's an erection, and death creeps forward the instant your dick bows its head in old age. If you don't believe this you are either dirt stupid or a liar. That night in the motel room UD tried to find a hooker. I'd like to get laid once more, he said, before I topple off the perch. After looking up escort services in the yellow pages he dialed a local number using the channel changer by mistake, wondering aloud why the teevee screen was flipping over and no one answered. They ought to show more respect, UD muttered, channel changer to his ear. I'm a potential customer. What is it with marketing people these days?

*O*ccasionally after the beach closed I went to Herb Feiler's Rip Tide Bar in Beach Haven. Herb was a short fat guy with slicked-back hair that lay on him like a dead raccoon facing wind. At happy hour he played an organ the size of a doomed church while singing poorly about dust from stars, journeys that were sentimental, and being taken out to ball games, and the blueheads clapped and sometimes wept from the grief of memory.

It was awful sitting there, but they served a happy hour special of a burger with a scoop of potato salad and bottle of beer for fifty cents. Two of these setups made a decent supper, and if you could wait it out Herb eventually moaned and organed himself to damp exhaustion and came down off the stage. Then Herb the

Celebrity would patter around the customers smiling lubriciously and offering a limp hand. Not long after, the disoriented, the lame, and those merely disabused of youth shuffled out, leaving the regulars to drink their dimies in peace.

We did most of our best work at Buckalews or at Britz's directly across the street, or the Acme on Dock Road by the bay, this last a legendary site where Bear Brown, having vowed to drown his girlfriend during a drunken argument, ushered her phantom presence into the passenger seat before driving his car down the boat ramp and barely escaping through an open window. He learned later that his girl had actually stayed behind, part of the cheering crowd. Today these places probably cater to yuppies wearing sport jackets and polished teeth, to young women who step demurely off curbs in sun dresses and white heels. I picture valet parking and flavored vodkas, chick food tasting of cellulose and starvation topped with a house vinaigrette.

Back then our bars had character. Viewed from outside, the Acme resembled a derelict barge sinking slowly into a swamp, although it looked that way from the inside too, just smokier. Its owners, Bird and Betty Clutter, were possibly born sad-faced and disgusted but more likely shifted that way after hearing someone speak the true frowning horror of their names. Their revenge was to stay busy at grim tasks hoping never to be hailed. Even in the slow morning times there was Betty methodically sweeping under the stools while Bird sterilized glasses by exhaling on the rims and rubbing off the steam with his greasy apron.

Several clammers drank regularly at the Acme, including Nelson Parker, self-proclaimed King of the Clammers. You clammed by wading barefoot and backward in the bay in waist-deep water pulling an inner tube with a basket or net inside. Upon feeling a clam you "treaded" it by sliding it up your leg using the other foot, then you reached down and grabbed it and tossed it into the tube.

Most clammers got a few hundred clams on a good day of low tide, but Nelson could tread two thousand without getting his chin wet and drink away the profit before midnight, going to bed too broke to buy gas for his pickup. Those times when the tide was with him Nelson could tread five thousand and then stay drunk for two days. One evening he came in with his legs scratched and bloodied after spending an hour shinnied up a piling while a dissatisfied shark circled underneath. Unfazed by the experience he showed his wounds all around. Them's from barnacles, he told us, not a whore's hangnail. But hugging that goddamn piling cut into my day's profit, so who's buying old Nelson his first dimie?

Freddy Dahl was usually on his customary stool by the door holding forth. He was a master of confused repartee. One night an attractive woman and her date were leaving when Freddy stopped her and said, I've been observing you all night, and you're alright by me. He then turned back to face the bar. In a voice rising as if from a pulpit, he said, Bird, another of your golden pilsners, and as payment please accept this dime earned by the sweat of my labors.

Another night the Acme was invaded by college jocks. They came in wearing those sleeveless undershirts to expose their arm muscles, what my daddy used to call eye-talian dinner jackets. They were self-impressed and bellowing like cattle, and one said he wanted to arm wrestle. He punched Freddy playfully on the shoulder and offered a challenge. Freddy was unnaturally strong despite the haunted stoop of the refugee and a chest that looked stepped on, and he put the kid's thick overfed arm down in seconds. All those curls and squats, those reps—my God, just the *pushups*. The kid was incredulous. Everyone stopped talking. In the silence Freddy said to him, Son, you should work on improving your mind, not your body. Then he announced to nobody in particular, When you've been in the dark a long time it takes a good light to find you.

After Jocker fired me I devoted an occasional hour of those empty days to a waitress named Trudy who poured coffee at Kapler's Drugstore. She was cute and bouncy and not letting me get close, although she liked to flirt. You never take me anywhere, she pouted, refilling my cup.

I'm always broke, I said. Why not simply debase ourselves in the wretched grief of sex? We can do that for free.

I'd rather not, she said.

Then I had an idea. Let's go clamming, I offered. We can sell the clams and make enough money for a date.

Do you know how to clam? she asked.

No, I said, but it can't be that hard.

The next morning Trudy, Cap, and I waded into Barnegat Bay carrying an inner tube with a gunny sack tied inside it. Cap had recently found employment in the distribution end of the clam business and figured it was time to learn something about production. His new job was driving a seafood truck around picking up "product" and delivering into downtown Philly and Fulton Fish Market in lower Manhattan. He had no license to drive an eighteen-wheeler, of course, and no experience either.

Cap told us about his first day while we sloshed around in the bottom muck feeling for clams with our toes. Cap had pressured the trucking company relentlessly, but the manager said he wasn't hiring. Finally the guy said to go see Hal in back of the building. Hal was a guy in his mid-eighties hobbling around the loading dock.

The boss says to see you about a job, said Cap.

Okay, Hal said, you can start now helping load this truck.

Are you the boss? Cap asked.

Sort of, Hal answered. I'm the owner. And when the truck's loaded you drive it around and pick up clams until it's full and then we go to Philly and unload. I got Parkinson's and can't drive anymore. Can't even smoke from the shaking. Goddamn cigarette ashes all over me. Burned up half my pants and most have holes I can piss through. That is, when I can piss at all.

After the truck was loaded Cap slid behind the wheel and Hal got in beside him, trembling and bobbing in the seat. That's reverse, Hal told him, and Cap promptly backed over the fence of a nearby tennis court. Hal stayed calm. Always test the brake first, he advised. On the highway the driving lesson continued. When you pull out of your lane to pass don't worry about oncoming vehicles, Hal said, because the car coming at you will always leave the road first, and remember not to think about the trailer. That's because where the cab goes the trailer follows, so pretend it ain't there.

Gears grinding, they lurched south through pines and low sand hills along narrow roads decorated with flattened wildlife. The old man gave occasional directions to turn here or there onto unmarked trails barely paved. At the first stop Cap backed into a clam shed with the owner standing there, partly crumpling the wall.

Hal said, Boy backed into your structure.

I noticed that, replied the piney.

Boy's got to learn, said Hal.

I agree, said the piney, but there's clam sheds up and down this road. Why'd you pick mine to go learn by?

Later they took on a load where two ancient pineys were sitting in the shade smoking pipes, friends of Hal's. Afternoon, Hal said.

Afternoon, they said back.

She's a hot one, Hal said.

She's a hot one, they agreed. Cap sat down with them to cool off while Hal checked the manifest.

What time be she? one piney asked the other.

Here she be, said the second piney holding out his watch.

Yup, there she be, said the first, neither of them knowing how to read the hands.

After a while one turned toward Cap. Boy, what time be she?

I got one! Trudy interrupted. I told her to tread it up. She tried, but it kept falling off her foot. I'll get it, I said, and ducked under. I pinched her toe, marveling at the quick response, then felt around and found the clam, which was actually a rock.

I surfaced and showed it to her saying, We can't sell this.

I've got another, she said, but it feels awfully smooth. I

retrieved the object, a jelly jar. She said, You guys are laughing, but I'll catch one eventually.

Eventually we all did. Cap and I got so we could slide a clam most of the way up a leg, but then the leg we were using as the slide got sore from being abraded by the rugose shells, so we tried to switch. It turns out that most people are either right-footed or left-footed clammers, having a natural inclination to grasp the clam with one or the other. Several nights later Nelson explained to us at great length how he eventually became proficient with either foot and soon stopped thinking about it. Ordinarily he wore a nylon stocking on one leg and slid the clam up that one with the other foot, which we knew already. When the clam hit his knee he popped it into the air and caught it. That lecture, delivered from a stool at the Acme, was unnecessarily windy, costing us two dimies for what had been a one-dimie question about clamming footedness.

Trudy's legs never got sore. When she felt a clam Cap or I was ordered to retrieve it, although she retained full credit for its capture. We worked all morning taking in a couple hundred clams. This is just great, Cap said. The wholesaler pays seventeen bucks a thousand, so what we got might be worth three or four bucks.

Well, I said to Trudy, at least we had a date, so let's go have sex.

This doesn't count as a date, she replied, splashing the mud off herself, but it's been fun clamming with you guys. She looked directly at me. Come see me when you want a real date. I have to go to work, don't you? She meant the diner.

Not until tonight, I replied. Meanwhile I think I'll be a clammer.

Cap and I took up clamming seriously, eventually getting about a thousand a day between us. Cap was also driving the seafood truck and I was working nights at the diner. If I needed extra money Hal hired me to help throw eighty-pound burlap sacks of wet clams into the truck trailer. We were flush. In the morning we hung out with the other clammers watching where

Nelson went, setting up near him and afterward selling the catch at a bayside pier. Later, after Jocker hired me back, I clammed only when broke, but Cap kept with it, eventually selling to Kapler's where the owner paid him extra to open those he used in the daily chowder. Pineys on the truck route had taught Cap the technique of inserting the knife blade near where the shells join and giving a sharp twist, and over the years he made a good buck opening clams at cocktail parties and restaurants.

*T*he Army had requested UD's presence in the summer of 1962. It pictured him in shaved head and khakis, polishing his brass and marching in dusty circles. In the Army's eyes he was practically saluting and saying yessir. It was just a matter of the paperwork. This new and hypothetical UD embraced early rising and personal hygiene, discipline, soldiering, and a chance to shoot honest-to-goodness bullets at some rice-eaters over in Asia who spoke a gibberish nobody understood. Nobody civilized, that is. They were gooks, what the hell.

But UD outflanked them. At his physical examination he and others were told to stand in a line and disrobe to their skivvies. UD was the only one naked.

I said to your *skivvies!* an Army-type person shouted in his face.

What are skivvies? asked UD.

At the interview he said he was queer and would love to join the Army, why had they waited so long to call. My, my, all those young farm boys with no carnal memories except of common barnyard stock and perhaps the chicken. Oh, he added, and I smoke mary-jew-wanna when I can get it and I'm not circumcised either. The Army doctor had told him thanks for coming over son, but we don't need your kind.

So UD, free of any commitments, was leaving for Mexico on his motor scooter, top speed thirty-five downhill at full throttle. Tied onto the back without forethought of balance were two changes of clothes, tenor sax and flute, pup tent and sleeping bag, camp cook set, dope and cigarettes in a waterproof bag, some groceries, English-Spanish dictionary, toenail clippers, and a toothbrush. He was hyped on bennies, jumping around inventing brilliant phrases and telling stories that kept us laughing. We somehow knew the trip was doomed, and maybe he did too.

Hey, he punched me, remember sitting on the stand at Holgate on the afternoon of the wasp? Oh man, *The . . . Afternoon . . . of . . . the . . . Wasp.* He turned to Cap. We're wearing standard issue short trunks and jock strap. One of my nuts has popped out, and suddenly a wasp lands on it. He—she, they're all female, it figures—climbs over and under and around for what seemed like hours but was really only a minute or two. Long enough. Aw, man! We're sitting there without a twitch, not even blinking, sweat running into our eyes, and finally the damn thing flies away. I turn to my partner here and says, The Lord punishes the wicked, and you crack up, remember? Har, har. Gawd-*damn*, weird stuff, I mean, life's got very strange, don't you guys think? Say something, fuckers! Anybody have a cig?

God, Cap and I loved him. Goodbyes and advice were dispensed on the Evelyn House steps. We mentioned road vibration and how it could weaken a man's resistance to masturbation. Think about the crabs, we cautioned, keep the pubes cut short, and forget those dysenteric rumors, it's okay to lap gutter water and lick vendor fruit. The girls in Mexico are clean, we added, not like Jersey skanks, so ride bareback and yippie-ki-oh. Mrs. Keating's eyes wetted up. Christ will watch over you, she called out, waving a hanky and thinking this was a scene in a papal documentary. Don't bet on it, we said, there's no salvation for the drunkard and the fornicator.

Two days later he was back distraught. It was early September, and that first night had been warm and clear when he camped along a country road. No need of a tent and sleeping bag, so he left everything tied to the scooter. He rolled a doobie, played the flute some sitting cross-legged and probably pounding out a little knee rhythm (bop-bidda-debop-*hoo*-debop-boom-*waaa*), fell asleep, and in the night thieves came along and stole everything except the clothes he was wearing, so he thumbed back to Beach Haven. We hugged him and told him that's a helluva way to start a road trip and what a pisser. Since you're back, want a beer?

    Of fucking course I do. Have I ever said I didn't want a beer?

    No, we agreed, you've never said that, but you surely are a dumbass.

    A few days later it was my time to leave. Cap and I subsequently saw each other over the years and even worked together in Connecticut in the seventies, but after shaking Uncle Dirty's hand I didn't see him again for forty-five years.

7

The year before, in 1961, following two semesters at college as a journalism student and the subsequent summer at Beach Haven, I hit the road, stimulated in part by lingering effects of Kerouac's novel but more so by the realization that journalism was incompatible with my objectives. Journalism, I had decided, was a process. It taught accuracy, succinctness, clarity, and directness—all useful tools—but it could never penetrate to those secret attributes of the conscious self that make every moment unique. As Graham Greene was to later write in *A Sort of Life*, the stitching of experiences into fiction is simply reporting, useful as background when the light falters, but what the writer *forgets* becomes, in Greene's words, the compost of the imagination.

A change was called for, and the choice was whether to be a writer of fiction or a scientist where I could seek some primal essence of life empirically. It was one or the other, no half-assed straddling a fence without visible ground on either side. Kerouac had composed *On the Road* during a frenzied writing binge over three weeks in April 1951, but only after struggling with previous versions for four years. The energy and madness burned through his prose, in Neal Cassady's strung-on conversations, the spoken equivalent of Charlie Parker's nonstop alto sax. The absence of commas and paragraph marks left the listener no resting place, the whole of it the conflagration of a pulsating soul.

I saw how Kerouac's words captured not just the harmonics and chromaticism of bebop, but its rhythmic discontinuity of startling brakes and acceleration: complex patterns of notes that zigzag like stepping stones across a rushing river. If you dismissed bebop's melodic contours then the prose read like careless gibberish. But in context with the music and the times it was electric; more important, it felt real. No writer spoke as he did, no other book had come at me this savage and immediate and stuck it in my eye like a blunt dirty finger. The moment had arrived to do something instead of sitting around comfortably thinking about it.

In early August I raised my thumb in Beach Haven and headed to Florida with forty dollars and a small bag holding a few belongings, mostly snorkeling gear. The previous winter Cap had quit college temporarily and worked in St. Thomas in the U.S. Virgin Islands. He returned with lots of exciting stories. I envied him and wished his stories had been mine because I loved hearing them told. There was a nearly irresistible urge to appropriate them, wallow in them, try them for fit like someone else's skin. What I needed were stories of my own if I was ever to write. The Virgin Islands seemed like a good place to reprise Cap's hiatus, although I would go to a different island, St. Croix, and get there by hitching a ride on a boat once I reached south Florida.

The trip was largely uneventful, and few details stick in memory. I stood around in sunshine and rain getting rides long and short, always asking to be dropped at truck stops where lifts were easy but you listened to a trucker's bullshit, often for hours, above the whine of diesel. Sometimes the drivers passed a pint my way and more rarely a sandwich. Lots of them were wired on speed, and the only way of keeping up was to beg a cap and cruise at their elevation. Occasionally during these episodes, if a trucker had let me out along a quiet road, I could hear my heartbeats shouting down the birds and cicadas, and instead of standing still I fidgeted among the roadside weeds looking sideways, expecting a banshee to come shrieking out of the tree line. Eventually the agitation and paranoia subsided, and I could wander into the bushes and nap for an hour.

I was shivering in a downpour in rural North Carolina when a shabby Volkswagen went by and stopped. I ran fast thinking it might squat permanently on the wet macadam, unable to rise again. Inside was a pale kid about my age, barely a ghost leaning out of the cigarette and marijuana smoke. Take a hit, he advised, extending his arm.

The rain phase-shifted to thick fog as we rattled slowly along the curvy two-lane road, the car ahead mostly visible as intermittent haloes of brake lights. Their blinking fixated us, mesmerized us, as we handed pre-rolled joints from his stash back and forth without speaking. Time went by, and the other car became a phantom to us both, unrecognized in the twilight for its true nature, like eyes that outshine and mask the leopard.

Then the lights blinked and veered in slow motion to the right. Abruptly a complete automobile came into view, motionless now, two of its wheels in a shallow ditch. Without even a glance the kid drove right through the silence. On we went, parting the gray cotton fog with no other vehicle ahead or behind, the wipers going swup, swup.

We must have driven ten miles before I said, Did you notice a car back there?

Yeah, he replied, You too? Man, that's weird.

I got to Ft. Lauderdale and found Pier 66, then touted as the world's largest yacht basin, which it maybe still is. After asking around I heard about a chartered sailboat leaving for St. Croix in a day or two. The crew was a hand short, and the captain said to come aboard right away. He offered a workaway's job—room, board, and passage, but no pay—and I accepted. I polished brass and oiled teak, cleaned the cabin heads, washed dishes, stood watch, and worked as a deck hand. The captain and mate rarely spoke to me, and the crew members kept to themselves, all of which was fine. The clients, an older couple, rarely appeared topside except at cocktail hour, preferring to stay in their cabin and read or listen to the short-wave.

I arrived at St. Croix with about fifteen dollars and no job. The first night I slept on a bench along King's Alley, but the second night the police came by and told me to move on. At dawn I came across a drunk Cruzan man who stopped me for a light. I asked if there was a cheap place to stay. He said I could bunk with him at a dollar a night and that my stuff would be safe. We went to his place, which was out Company Street where the town sank in stature, becoming low buildings and shacks. His lodgings off an alley comprised a room furnished by two bare mattresses on the floor. They were stained and filthy. Tucked into a corner was a toilet and tiny stall shower with water that dribbled continuously from the showerhead. I took a shower, which dribbled a little stronger with the faucet turned on. Fleas were hopping around on the mattress. I was too tired to care and went to sleep.

Late that afternoon I wandered into town and ended up at the Stone Balloon, a bar inside a windmill built by the Dutch, whose ownership of the island had ended in 1917. The urinal in the men's room was out of order. It contained a bouquet of artificial roses and a note to please piss in the sink. On the other side of the wall of the barroom, accessible through a large rectangular opening, was a Christian Science reading room. You could get a rum and Coke at the bar for thirty-five cents, which consisted mostly of rum because Coke was more expensive.

I was having a drink when a large heavy man walked in and sat down beside me. He was American, dressed entirely in white and wearing a white Panama like a plantation owner of the Old South, which he was, sort of. He ordered a drink, bought me one, and we began to converse. His name was Mr. Benzner, and he was from Alabama.

He said there were only a few white men on the island who didn't have jobs on boats or the few hotels and he was looking for someone to supervise his Cruzan crew in the cane fields. There was still some sugarcane being grown then, and it needed to be cut by hand, loaded onto his two trucks, and brought into town to the dock. Mr. Benzner asked if I might be interested in being the overseer. I said I was and accepted the job at wages of twenty-five dollars a week.

Be at the corner of King's Cross and Company streets at six o'clock, he said, when the trucks came through town rounding up men looking for a day's work. One of the drivers would be a Cruzan named Albert who, according to Mr. Benzner, was the only trustworthy nigger around. Albert would be my second in command.

I bought a loaf of bread, some canned meat, and cigarettes, then returned to the room and went to bed. My roommate was out drinking and came in the next morning just as I was leaving. He seemed to remember our arrangement, and after I gave him several cigarettes and a dollar he thanked me and passed out on his mattress.

The trucks, which were dump trucks, came by on time. I could hear them coughing and backfiring several blocks away. There were eight or so Cruzan laborers riding in the bed of each and two more in the cabs. I waved, and they stopped. A Cruzan got out of the passenger side of the lead truck and swung up into the bed. I got in and met Albert. He smiled, and we shook hands, already sweating in the coming heat of the day. On the floor of the cab were some machetes and a couple of whetstones, and Albert said there were more machetes in the truck beds.

So you the new overseer, mon? and he laughed in a friendly way.

That's me, I replied, which made him laugh even harder. We bumped out of town and into the hinterland, lurching past roadside shacks and maize patches, swerving to avoid strolling goats and burros. Roosters crowed behind laundry that hung tiredly from sagging lines. In back of us the crew sang enthusiastically, the lead singer shouting something melodic that became a refrain for the rest of the chorus. I was feeling good.

Albert yelled out something to the crew through his open window and pulled off the road into a field of stubble. We bounced a hundred yards or so until an imposing wall of sugarcane rose into view, then turned around and backed the trucks up to it. Everyone jumped out. I figured it was best not to ask questions and look stupid. My plan was to walk authoritatively back and forth in front of the canebrake watching the workers chop down the stalks and haul them to the trucks. The sun would not be a problem because I was already deeply tanned from summer at the beach.

The men stood around in a group as if waiting for something. They ranged from middle-school age to old men gray in the hair. I stepped forward. Okay, I barked, let's attack that line and cut some cane. Albert here will pass out machetes. I think they're already sharp, but if not we have whetstones in the cab. They started to laugh, slapping their thighs and giving each other wide-eyed looks. I turned to Albert, and he was laughing too. After a time they picked up the machetes and wandered languidly toward the canebrake.

I caught up with Albert. Why's everybody laughing? I asked.

Because you funny, mon. Them boys knows how to cut cane, they be cutting cane many a year now. They thinking it funny you acting like a baas.

But I *am* the boss, I protested.

Yass baas, he said, doubling over. He started to giggle uncontrollably, holding his midsection and stumbling about as if unable to stand.

Thinking to lead by example I got a machete and joined the line hacking at the base of this quivering forest, but my effort seemed unnoticed. The singing commenced led by one man whose words were flung back at him by the rest. I chopped along at a good pace, noticing how the sugary sap mingled with my sweat, matting the arm hairs into sticky swirls. The fibrous stalks were twelve feet tall and packed closely together. I felt like a bug on an overgrown lawn. The crew, in contrast, chopped with desultory strokes using just enough energy to gain total cleavage. Each stalk was then cut to lengths that would fit in the trucks. We handed these up to men in the beds who arranged them in orderly rows to conserve space.

I didn't have a watch, but after about two hours, maybe a little longer, everyone stopped simultaneously, walked over to a large breadfruit tree in the field, and lay down underneath it. This was when I noticed the water jugs. We poured the water into cups and passed them around, everyone sucking down the contents in silence. Afterward the men stretched out in the shade.

I went over and tapped Albert. Shouldn't we get back to work? I asked.

He giggled. It hot, mon, you not feel the sun? You got to be careful, that sun cook you like an egg.

It's hot every day, I replied.

No baas, it more hotter today. Today is a very hot day, very dangerous. He rolled onto his side and closed his eyes, showing only the back of his head and bottoms of his calloused feet placed one atop the other.

I climbed onto one of the truck beds and looked inside, seeing it was filled to only about quarter capacity. The metal of the bed was nearly too hot to touch. I went back underneath the tree and sat down beside Albert, who was already snoring. Some of the men talked quietly. I lit a cigarette and passed around the pack, practically full. It didn't come back. That pissed me off.

Okay, I said sternly, everybody back to work. They only glanced my way before resuming conversations. Screw it, I thought, and lay down too. The day was windless, so quiet that anoles scurrying through the brown grass sounded huge and dangerous. Ants were thick on the ground and running up and down the tree, and soon they were actively seeking the sugar crystallizing on our skin and clothes. I dozed off dripping with ant spit, understanding vaguely how a lactating aphid must feel.

After sleeping most of the day we got up, stretched, climbed into the trucks, and drove back toward town, stopping occasionally to drop men off along the way. Mr. Benzner was waiting at the dock looking like a vanilla ice cream sundae topped by a hat. He waved and gestured as the trucks backed up and dumped their loads. This is all you cut? he asked me.

Everyone knocked off in the morning, I said, and went to sleep under a tree.

Jesus Christ, son, it's your job to see that don't happen. These lazy bastards ain't likely to work unless you kick their ass. They snookered you.

I think Albert put them up to it, I said.

Then you needed to kick Albert's ass. He don't appreciate supervision, and that's his way of making you go away. And you just did. Here's fifteen dollars. Go on, take it, he said, waving the bills at me. You're fired.

There was a place in town where they sold a thick sandwich for fifty cents. I was chewing on one of these and walking around the dock when a native sloop came about at the harbor entrance and tacked expertly among the anchored vessels. The skipper, a wrinkled older man with grizzled hair and beard, dropped the sail at the last second, and the boat eased up to the dock without raising a ripple. Whoever this guy was he played first chair in seamanship's great symphony.

I walked over and saw that the boat was built of heavy timber. It was beamy and entirely open, about twenty-five feet, rigged simply with a single sail, and steered with a tiller in the stern. The mate was young, maybe my age. He jumped onto the dock and nimbly tied off while the old man pulled and wrapped the sail. The cargo consisted entirely of sacks of coconuts and baskets of produce. There were island tomatoes and stubby ears of maize, peppers, squashes, breadfruits, mangoes, papayas, bananas.

I finished the sandwich and pitched in, receiving items the old man lifted onto the dock and setting them down beside a pickup that appeared suddenly. Two native women were sliding the stuff into a predetermined arrangement around the truck.

They laughed and joked with the old man, telling him he was late as usual, asking if he had a girlfriend over there. At his age, they said, everything took longer, which could explain why he hadn't arrived yesterday as scheduled. He received the jibes good-naturedly and gave some back, saying that were either of them his girlfriend he would have nothing except time on his hands. They found this hilarious. The younger guy remained silent and unsmiling, lugging baskets and sacks with his skinny arms, stepping over things in his bare oversized feet.

The old man thanked me when we finished. I asked where they were coming from. St. Thomas, he said. He and his nephew freighted produce that came into Charlotte Amalie on St. Thomas from the bigger islands like Puerto Rico and Hispaniola, and a couple of small wholesalers on St. Croix paid him to bring it over. The two ladies sold most of it right at the dock to residents and chefs from the hotels and restaurants. He gave me two bananas, and I scarfed them on the spot laughing inwardly. A monkey's wages, I thought.

He told me his name was Clifford. His nephew was unable to make the next trip, and he asked if I could mate over and back. He might be able to pay me a few dollars. We could be gone a week starting tomorrow, but less time if the good weather held. I said okay.

With the outgoing tide? I asked. He looked confused, then caught on and laughed.

No, baas, he said, no tide. We leave tomorrow morning when there's wind. I asked about food. He said he would bring the food and drink but I might need a heavy shirt because the nights could get cold, especially if it rained.

He showed me a couple of old blankets folded and wrapped in plastic if we needed them, and two battered oilskin jackets with hoods. There were no life preservers, flashlights, or flares, no floatation or signaling devices of any sort. If the boat sank we were basically screwed. Our single instrument was a handheld compass, which he displayed proudly, tapping on the scratched lens to make the needle move.

Clifford showed up the next morning wearing yesterday's clothes, although we had dressed similarly. Like him I was barefoot in grubby shorts and t-shirt with a baseball cap on my head. Unlike him I was carrying a sweatshirt. In my pockets were cigarettes and matches and the few dollars I owned. Empty, the boat seemed the size of a barge. I untied us and pushed the bow away from the dock. Clifford raised the sail, and we were ponderously underway. It must have been about seven o'clock. He steered adroitly among expensive sailboats and native craft dotting the harbor. The northeast trade wind required that we tack to open water. It was a masterful display of sailing, and I stayed out of the way as Clifford operated the tiller with one hand and continuously repositioned the boom with the other.

Outside the harbor the trades were steady at about ten knots. Charlotte Amalie was forty miles north, but tacking increased the distance. Assuming the wind held, we would arrive late that night. Clifford tied down the boom, threw one leg over the tiller, and opened his thermos of black coffee. He poured some into the cap and we passed it back and forth. There was fruit from yesterday and bread and jam. Afterward I supplied cigarettes and we settled back to watch the frigate birds soaring like winged daggers high overhead. Our starting tack seemed to be north-northwest and some spray came over the starboard gunnels as the boat labored through low swells, but it felt refreshing, and whenever water struck Clifford full in the face he laughed as if nature had played a huge joke on him.

I suppose I was expecting sea stories, at the least something similar to Santiago's abbreviated thoughts in *The Old Man and the Sea*. Clifford, however, was disinclined to talk, and I remembered that his nephew had been withdrawn too. These were no doubt silent passages. Clifford had not once looked at his compass, and land was nowhere in sight. I asked him how he knew which way to steer.

I know which way the wind come, he replied, and I remember the position of the sail.

Yes, but the wind can change a few degrees, and then you'd need to change the sail's position.

Yass, baas, he said, but I can tell when the wind change. My eyes is not good now, I see in a fog, but I can feel the wind on my face like the kiss of a pretty woman. You got a cigarette? I lit two cigarettes and passed him one. It was true about his eyes, which were clouded with cataracts.

I been sailing the islands since I'm a small boy. He held his hand out palm down about three feet off the deck. About so high, he laughed. I used to sail all over with my father and brothers, but my father died and the brothers took to farming. Now the boat is mine, and I sail only to St. Thomas and back. It used to be that boats like this brought many things to St. Croix, but today not so much. We have airplanes and island freighters, so I carry produce, which people like to eat fresh.

Do you buy it yourself? I asked.

No, the agents over there buy it. I just carry it.

Same as a floating truck driver, I said.

Yes! he exclaimed. He slapped his knee and laughed. A floating truck driver, that's me. He adjusted the sail and looked to the sky as if hopeful of clear vision.

So this boat must be pretty old, I offered. It was a statement.

Yass, baas, very old, even older than me, and I am fifty-six coming this year. My father and grandfather built it. But it's well made, you know? It needs very little maintenance. About every six months my nephew and I haul it out with my brother's tractor. Then we scrape the bottom and caulk the leaks, but we put it back quickly so the boards stay swelled, you know? He chuckled and said, You ask a lot of questions.

The sun and salt and wind had long since wrinkled Clifford's skin, sucking out the youthful moisture until he looked much older than his stated age, but he moved spryly taking care of this or that. Once he asked me to hold the tiller while he jumped to coil deck lines near the bow. Tiller in hand I could feel the boat's sturdy mass as it carved the swells without the exaggerated roll and pitch you sometimes felt aboard fiberglass vessels.

We were sailing through indigo water on a day of fierce sunlight, a breeze blowing down and across us, cooled by soft spray. The boat's rhythmic heave and the blue sky made everything magical. We crossed the paths of flying fishes, and they sprang like grasshoppers from the slopes of the swells, hitting the sail and falling to the deck. We gathered them up, sprinkled hot pepper sauce on them, and ate them raw. Clifford played out a line baited with a flying fish, and soon we had a small dorado aboard. It too became sashimi. We finished off with a swallow each of rum and a cigarette, watching the sun grow large and oblate. It all made you feel small in the day.

It was well after dark when we got to Charlotte Amalie, but Clifford steered through the maze of boats and moorings directly to the dock, where we tied off to a line of truck tires hanging against the seawall. I will be gone two days, he said. My wife is waiting. Please stay with the boat late at night. There are vandals. He disappeared into the crowd.

I walked into town and bought a used paperback novel, a quart of rum, a bottle of cold beer, and a sandwich. Charlotte Amalie was bigger and livelier than Christiansted. People were out and about laughing and talking in the streets; they sat on porch steps and curbs and benches drinking from bottles and smoking. Sounds of recorded calypso and live steel bands escaped through the open doors and windows of bars, interesting in context, although I've never liked Caribbean music. After two or three hours of wandering I returned to the boat. The harbor lights were too dim to read by, so I took a couple of swallows of rum and wrapped up in one of Clifford's blankets. It smelled of tired wood and sea salts and the ancient drift of plankton.

Over the next couple of days I read, napped, and walked around town, stopping to watch wealthy Americans and Europeans being ferried ashore from their yachts to fancy restaurants, the women sunburned in their thin dresses and jewelry, the men ruddy and blustery. They stepped carelessly over the drunk and homeless, picking their way around gutted sacks of garbage and lumps of dog shit. The populace largely ignored them, hopping to street music, accosting friends with shouted greetings and friendly insults. Here were parallel universes sliding past each other, colliding briefly with a nearly impalpable friction—an order to a boatman, instructions to a cabbie or maid—then each party dissolved into its own world invisible to the other. And there I was in the wonder of simplicity, happy owning nothing and watching everyone without envy. It was so easy to shit over the gunnels, to lie back and be rocked to sleep, to pull and secure a line and know you were now going in a different direction. Shower? The dock hose; bring your own soap.

When Clifford returned the morning of the third day we began loading the boat with produce. He knew exactly where each item was to be placed for proper balance. Loading took all day, interrupted periodically while Clifford sought out dealers of this or that. Nothing happened quickly or efficiently. He understood everyone's quirks and failings. When the seller of tomatoes failed to appear Clifford figured he was drunk at a certain bar and went off to find him. He knew that a dealer in papayas and mangoes would sell his fruits elsewhere if a higher price were offered. Someone said the coconut man would be late and maybe not come at all, but he did, eventually.

What about the agents? I asked. Don't they tend to this so you don't have to?

Yass, baas, except the agents don't do their job.

We slept aboard that night and left early the following morning, this time running before the wind. The return trip was hotter with the wind behind us, and sometimes we doused our shoulders with seawater. The boat rode lower now and seemed to wallow. I asked about his wife.

Which wife? he replied.

You have more than one?

Yass, baas, I have two wife, one St. Thomas, one St. Croix.

You dog, I said.

He laughed and slapped his thigh. Yass, you see, the wife St. Thomas make a good goat stew, the wife St. Croix she cook seafood very good. You know what I mean? A man has got to eat right or he become weak.

We unloaded at St. Croix while the two cackling women rearranged every load I brought them. When we finished Clifford handed me a water-soaked five-dollar bill and thanked me. He said his nephew would be coming back to work with him. I thanked him too and said I'd be seeing him around.

I got a local paper and read in the classifieds that Grapetree Bay Hotel on the far eastern end of the island needed a lifeguard. Previous experience required, the ad said, room and board included. It paid forty-five dollars a week. I went to where my things were stored, showered, put on the cleanest clothes I had, and thumbed east.

The assistant manager was a young American wearing horn-rimmed glasses and dressed in a jacket and tie. We talked a few minutes, and he hired me. I'll get one of the drivers to take you into town to get your stuff, he said, as we were walking to the dorm. It was a single-storey concrete block building with a hall in the center, rooms on both sides, and music coming from everywhere.

Each room had two bunks, and there were showers and toilets at the ends of the halls. The floors were poorly finished concrete, the walls unpainted cinder block. The women lived in a similar dorm nearby. There was no air conditioning, but the air seemed cool enough without it. He opened a door. You can stay in here, he said. Looks like someone's already using that bunk, so take this one. We serve breakfast, lunch, and supper to the help over there, he said, pointing through the window to another building. Times are posted at the entrance. Now let's review the duties.

There was little to do. In the morning I arranged furniture in pleasing symmetry on the large deck around the pool and set out towels. Using the long-handled net I scooped out any dead insects floating at the surface, emptied and cleaned the overflow trap to the filter, and got into the pool to pick out any large items. The covered part of the deck included an outdoor bar and bandstand, and sometimes on Sunday mornings there were high-heeled sandals floating in the water and rarely a bra or panties. I often recovered cocktail glasses from the bottom, nearly invisible against the pale blue paint. If any had broken I put on mask and flippers and swept up what pieces I could see using a whisk broom and dustpan. I was on duty six days a week, mostly just watching the bathers, fetching towels, and rearranging chairs and chaises. The deck overlooked the ocean, but hardly anyone walked down there, and if they took a swim they were on their own.

My first day off I went into town with one of the drivers who was picking up a shipment at the dock and walked around looking into store windows until I found a place that sold junk and anything used. I bought an old Underwood typewriter in a carrying case and several new ribbons. Hotel business was slow until the tourist season, so I set the typewriter on a table with a clear view of the pool and did some writing during the day. The assistant manager came by once and told me it was okay to do this now, but not when things got busy. I wrote every afternoon for a couple of hours, stories mostly, but also the beginning of a novel. The rest of the time I sat trying to think of things to write about.

My roomie was a Haitian gardener with lots of gold teeth and skin the color of charcoal. He smiled a lot, although we could barely communicate. Everyone else in the dorm was Cruzan or Puerto Rican, and they all wore different colognes. The scents jousted and circled one another, pounced and hybridized. Entering the building was like walking into an exotic tropical whorehouse. One of the guys had made a set of barbells by sticking the ends of iron pipes into cement-filled cans of different sizes. In the evenings we sometimes lifted weights and drank beer, cheering and urging each other on.

A Puerto Rican gardener named Angel bunked across the hall and became a sort of sidekick. We ate together at the big table in the staff dining room, endless meals of rice and beans. Angel had been in the Army paratroops, to which every conversation ultimately returned as if magnetized. It had been the high point of his life and now, he said, he was a fucking gardener for some soft white tourists. What a comedown, but when it rained the plants grew and it was job security. The vegetable kingdom was Angel's enemy, green and skulking and needing discipline. Disregarding hotel protocol he wore full fatigues and a fatigue cap and strode daily onto his field of battle to face down recalcitrant regiments of hibiscus and oleander. Each week he took more ground, and each week the rear guard lost it again.

You can't trust the Haitian, he told me, meaning my roomie. We were standing outside the dining room after lunch.

Why not? I asked.

Because he's not just a nigger, he's a Haitian. He'll steal from you.

One of his gold teeth is worth more than everything I own.

You'll find out, dumbass. What's that tree again? I need to learn them.

That one? A queen palm.

A queen palm? Jesús Cristo. I suppose there's also a king palm.

There is, and a princess palm too. Angel dropped the butt he was smoking and stomped it under the heel of his combat boot.

They all look the same, he said, like fucking Haitians. So how can you tell them apart?

I pointed up. That one has fronds like a feather, that one over there like a palm, the palm of a hand (*la palma de la mano*).

He lit another cigarette and squinted at me. Cut it out, okay? No shapes and stuff, just explain how to tell them apart.

Talk to me in Spanish, I advised him one day. From then on our conversations took the form of Angel watching skeptically as I bumbled along. The Spanish professor back at college was an imperious Catalonian from Barcelona. To him the New World had bastardized the language of his heritage. Spanish-speaking residents of the Western hemisphere were illiterates, imbeciles with tortured tongues mouthing sounds like a wrinkle unfolding.

He insisted on Castilian pronunciation and raged at us for demeaning it with our hillbilly accents. Angel's Spanish sounded very different from his. I started naming things in his presence: *lagarto* (lizard), *arbol* (tree), *césped* (grass), *bicho* (bug) . . . . *Bug?* Angel doubled over. Bug! Ha! *Bicho* means *penis* in Puerto Rico. That thing, that crawling thing, is *el insecto*. Period. *No es el bicho*. If you tell me, *Yo se lo metí a ella*, I'll naturally be thinking it was your dick you stuck in her—your *bicho*—not a damn bug. So don't talk like a *pendejo*, and don't ever call a Puerto Rican *pendejo* unless you know him, okay? Something like that happened to me in Airborne. This guy I barely knew says to me, Hey *pendejo*, and I. . . .

The piano player in the bar was an American named Ralph Martin who had a degree in music from the University of Miami. He lived with his wife and little daughter in one of the apartments the hotel maintained on the grounds. His brother was Don Martin, the cartoonist for *Mad* magazine. He told me Don had a degenerative eye condition and didn't know how much longer he could continue drawing his outrageously funny cartoons.

Ralph's job at cocktail hour was to play tunes everyone knew so they could sing along, but what he really wanted was to write and play jazz. He was a fan of Bill Evans. Ralph's wife Betty was a sweet woman who wrote pornographic novels under a pseudonym. I asked to read one hoping to learn how she went about constructing a book, but she was too embarrassed. I never did find out her nom de plume or the titles of any of her works. She told me only that she was paid a lump sum for the manuscripts and received no royalties.

Ralph wanted to visit Haiti and write down the drum rhythms coming out of the mountains. They were wild, he said to me one day by the pool. Man, think about working those into a jazz piece for piano. Just a Bill Evans-type trio: piano, drums, and bass. What a gas. Ralph was only in his thirties but already had snow-white hair. He looked at me with eyes so pale blue they seemed depthless.

Okay, I said.

Business was still slow, and after a couple of weeks I finagled four days off, and Ralph and I flew to Port-au-Prince by way of San Juan. With room and board free, I had money to spare. When we got there we told a taxi driver about wanting to hear nighttime drumming that came from the hills. The guy said sure, he knew about it, and he also knew a cheap place to stay outside town, a couple of bucks a night. There were some food shacks around. They closed early and then things were quiet.

He drove us into the boondocks along rutted roads to an old woman's house set among a small cluster of similar houses and tiny stores and food shacks. She spoke no English, but the room she offered had two clean beds, a toilet, and an outside shower surrounded by a plastic curtain. The driver said he could come back at a prearranged time and take us to the airport.

We set down our bags and went over to one of the little stores and bought a cold six-pack. A teenager loafing by the door asked if we wanted any marijuana and maybe a couple of whores. We said sure to the first and bought some from him, along with a package of rolling papers. Ralph declined a whore, but I didn't. The kid came around an hour later with a slender girl about sixteen. He told me she understood the situation and how much I was to pay her, which was five dollars a day.

For the next two days the three of us stayed mostly stoned, lying in hammocks stretched between coconut palms. The girl, who was sweet and friendly, fetched beers for us from the food stands and spent considerable time giggling and trying to communicate with me in Creole. If I failed to respond she seemed distraught, so occasionally I laughed or smiled and nodded my head. I soon saw the unintended consequences. Now thinking I understood she became even more animated, jabbering nonstop and climbing into the hammock and hugging me.

Ralph had brought along a thick tablet of staff paper for writing music, and at night we fired up joints, popped cold beers, and listened to the fantastic drumming that seemed to slide down onto us from the sky. I knew I should be making notes of a more conventional sort but felt disinclined. As a result Ralph returned from the trip with a working notebook; I had nothing except a few foggy memories. For days I heard him composing at the piano while I was trying to write by the pool. He was an artist already formed, trained to snatch notes out of the air and transcribe them—air music—while I composed stories that seemed increasingly banal and poorly written. I was envious of Ralph, not just of his talent but his skill and focus. I felt I was lounging around in someone else's moment.

8

Cap was back in college so I sent UD a postcard care of his parents in New Jersey. It depicted a girl in a bikini with palms in the background. They forwarded it to Sarasota, Florida, where he was rooming temporarily with a high school buddy who worked as a city cop. He fired off a reply as soon as the card arrived, advising me to stay put, that he was on the way after scrounging the needed travel money. He figured on hopping a bus to Miami and a plane from there.

A week later he showed up by the pool. I took him to see the assistant manager, who gave him a kitchen job as pot washer. We moved into a room together in the dorm. The story about staying with an old buddy had been a ruse; actually he had been living with a divorced woman in Sarasota who was pregnant. The baby was due any day, so my postcard arrived at a good moment. It was time to quit riding the hump, he said. Although the kid was her ex-husband's, she had been half expecting UD to stick around and play the daddy.

Sitting by the pool all day was boring, and I suggested to the assistant manager that we take guests snorkeling in front of the hotel and charge them a fee for the experience. The reefs were close to shore. He liked the idea and ordered in masks, flippers, and snorkels. We set up designated snorkeling times on specific days and posted signs at the pool saying no lifeguard would be on duty during those hours. UD started coming along on the afternoon jaunts after finishing up in the kitchen. There were huge fishes everywhere. Man, he said after first seeing the reef, we could make some tough bread spearing fish and peddling them to the hotels. I told him there was a fish market in town at the dock where selling them might be easier. Let's do it, he said.

I snorkeled over the reefs, enchanted and astounded. Marine biology was a new field, and books on the subject were few. For pure rapture there was *Diving to Adventure* by Hans Hass and Guy Gilpatric's *The Compleat Goggler*, both of which I had bought and read while at boarding school. They occupy my library shelves to this day, and every so often I blow the dust off one or the other and read it again. But no prose descriptions matched being there in the silence immersed in a maelstrom of flashing colors. Each day brought new insights, new information, new wonders. Life out there was mobile and congested, making it hard to concentrate on individual fishes and invertebrates and try to figure out what they were doing.

I cruised the reefs at dawn and dusk and when time permitted during the workday and would gladly have gone at night, but underwater flashlights had not yet been developed. There were no field guides, but I could recognize such general groups as angelfishes, butterflyfishes, groupers, grunts, and squirrelfishes. I could distinguish some of the prominent corals and noted that certain ones grew at predictable depths. I learned the lobsters, a few of the other large crustaceans, and some of the sea anemones. Reef sharks occasionally glided beneath me close to the reef. I was hooked, and knew if I ever worked in the life sciences it could only be as a marine biologist.

We quit our jobs at the hotel and moved into a single room with two beds and a bathroom on Hospital Street in Christiansted across from the police station. The rent was forty-five dollars a month. I forget how much fish and conch were selling for, but enough to make the venture potentially profitable. Furthermore we could fish when we wanted and kick back after accumulating some money. We figured that working every day was for suckers. And what could be better than being out on the reef? It was perfect.

Before UD arrived I had done some exploring of the coast and found a cove east of Grapetree Bay where someone had stashed a beat rowboat among the rocks. I took it out two or three times, dropping over the stone anchor and snorkeling across grassy pastures of grazing conchs. On the first day of new freedom UD and I thumbed out there carrying snorkeling equipment, a burlap bag, and a machete. In two hours we filled the bag with conch meat, caught a ride back to Christiansted with some field workers, and sold our catch at the dock. There was enough for groceries and to put toward the next month's rent. We celebrated by buying a quart of Cruzan rum and getting drunk.

We started hanging around the Stone Balloon at night, getting to know the regulars. Among them was René, a thin bonynosed Frenchman who described himself as self-employed, although exactly what this meant was unclear. René had memorable breath and a habit of talking close in your face while looking side to side as if someone nearby might actually be listening. When not speaking he whistled absently through his teeth, producing the tuneless noises of a failed bird shuffling toward extinction. But his enthusiasm was what grabbed you.

René said he was from Marseilles and had worked his way around the world on boats of all sizes, everything from open sloops to ocean liners. He was friendly and charming, and the women told their husbands or boyfriends they should act more like René because he really knew how to treat a lady. They loved his accent. Even better, he listened intently when they talked, as if no one else mattered. He kissed the backs of their hands, tossed off compliments that seemed passably sincere, and pulled out chairs and opened doors. Not surprisingly, René, or the past or future presence of René, often became a subject of lusty familial arguments.

One evening René seemed quieter than usual, sad and not whistling. He told us there were personal problems without elaborating. He lowered his head, sighed mightily, readjusted the world on his shoulders, and returned to sipping from a glass of wine. We asked if we could help, but he shook his head, staring into the wine and twirling the glass in a slow philosophical way as if each movement portended some awful calamity.

I need money, he said without hope, and you guys are broke too. We offered to lend twenty bucks if that helped, and his expression rose an inch or two above melancholy. To us this was a fortune. He grabbed both our hands and thanked us several times. Others in the bar chipped in. He was our friend, and he was hurting.

René disappeared the next day, no one knew where. We figured, okay, he shafted us, but lesson learned. His absence was hotly discussed at the Balloon, the conversation fueled by high humidity and cheap alcohol, with some patrons even foregoing the month-old newspapers in the next room.

Charming, yeah, and pulled out a chair for you? a guy would say sarcastically to his wife or girlfriend. What did I tell you all along? I don't mean to rub your nose in this. On the other hand. . . .

Even Mr. Benzner was pissed, having extended René the kingly sum of a hundred dollars. He could pass off that strutting of the Cruzans as mere habit correctable by American discipline, but René . . . now René was different entirely considering there was no available cure for being foreign. Mr. Benzner spent evenings sipping highballs, Panama on the bar sopping up condensation, wiping his large red face with an even larger white handkerchief and muttering to himself.

A week later René returned wearing new clothes and moving under scented hair oil. He came into the Balloon with a thick stack of cash folded over, paid everyone back, and bought us drinks. We were astounded. What a relief, he told us, to have friends like you, genuine friends who help in times of emergency. We slapped his back and said how good it was having him around again. The women gave him sympathetic glances while the men hunched furtively, seeing sheepish reflections in their drinks.

A couple of weeks went by and again René became distraught. This time when UD and I talked to him he clutched our arms and wept. The Balloon turned silent. It was heart-wrenching to see someone you liked in such agony. He told us he was unable to eat or sleep, and indeed he appeared thin and haggard with gray tips on his stubble. This remaining obligation was too great a burden; he had no idea what to do. He needed money badly but his friends were under no pressure, having saved him once. That had been all the generosity anyone could expect. . . . His voice trailed off. He looked toward the wall and waved us away with Gallic flips of the wrist.

Nonsense, we said. Give us a couple of days. Everyone ran around gathering up what he could spare. UD and I produced fifty dollars, every bit of cash we had, which included most of the future rent. Others gave more, some much more. René thanked us profusely and wept again, causing the women and not a few of the men to weep with him. He left after dispensing hugs and handshakes, saying he'd be back in a week, but it was a wonderful con. We never saw him again.

UD and I invested in our fishing business by purchasing two double-stranded arbaletes, powerful spear guns with which to slay even bigger fishes. We were in terrific condition. I was free diving to seventy feet or so, spearing a fish, and bringing it to the surface, often staying submerged for three minutes while actively searching for a fish to shoot. UD was adept with the gun but unable to dive as deep. Between us we covered a wide swath of reef effectively. Because the Cruzans ate anything from the sea we were even spearing large rainbow parrotfishes that patrolled the shallower water in schools, stopping intermittently to crunch algae growing on the dead corals. Some of these weighed nearly thirty pounds. We also carried heavy work gloves with which to grab spiny lobsters and drag them out from underneath ledges.

There was never a problem selling the catch. In late afternoon the fish market was crowded with Cruzans buying something for the evening meal and hotel chefs filling out the day's menu. Lobsters brought in the most money followed by conchs, groupers, and snappers. We learned to distinguish the different fishes, knowing that certain species were preferred by the professional chefs.

Usually we left early in the morning and thumbed out to places where we could climb down the rocky slopes to the water. Often lunch was some of the catch cooked on a driftwood fire. A Cruzan guy had taught us how lobsters could be cooked by simply throwing them into hot coals until they blackened. Then you raked them out and cracked open the shells. The meat had a smoky taste, perfect with a squeeze of lime juice. We always carried a machete for cleaning conchs, but it was also handy for opening coconuts to get the milk and meat. After a short rest we went back into the water for another hour or so, usually finishing up by mid-afternoon when it was easy to hitch rides in the trucks taking field workers back to town, especially if you offered the driver a fish.

We were spearfishing one day and doing well when truth confronted me. It was one of those large truths requiring major decisions, the kind that lurk out of sight and stay away so long you forget about them, then suddenly they jump in front of you, big and hairy and frightening. When UD and I got to the beach I told him.

This is it for me, I said. The writing isn't coming along well. In fact, it stinks. I came down here to see if writing was plan A and it didn't work out, so now it's plan B. He asked what plan B was, and I said science. I was going to be a scientist, which meant I had to stop screwing off and get back in school.

After we sold the day's catch I nosed around the dock and asked at the Balloon, but no one knew of a boat leaving for the States. I suggested to UD that if he was coming along we ought to get over to Charlotte Amalie where there was more action. He said, I'm coming with you baas. It took a couple of days to square up debts and get rid of some things we no longer needed, then we used most of our money to buy plane tickets and hopped over to St. Thomas.

Cap had told me of a bar called Katie's, owned by an overweight dyke who wore too much makeup and played the piano. Cap said you could sleep there and nobody cared. The first night UD and I slept on benches by the harbor and in the morning started asking around about a boat. Nothing was leaving. We went to Katie's. Her place was dark and woody and furnished with wide futons, each the size of a single bed. The clientele consisted mostly of gays and lesbians snuggling and making out while Katie played and sang. We bought a couple of drinks and waited around until closing, at which point Katie took the drawer out of the cash register, waved goodbye, and left. You could go behind the bar and make yourself a drink or just go to sleep. We did one and then the other.

The following morning I telephoned the St. Thomas *Daily News* and asked about any jobs that might be available. My call was passed through to someone who asked what I was seeking, and I said a position in journalism. I said I could write clearly, type about eighty words a minute, and had completed one year of journalism college. She said that was perfect, they needed someone and could I come over right away. I found the offices and waited an hour until a secretary said the editor could see me. He got up to shake my hand, but seemed surprised.

You didn't tell my secretary you were white, he said.

She didn't ask, I replied. Well, he said, you're qualified for the reporter's job, but everyone here in the office is black, and I'm in no position to hire a white man. Sorry. He looked down at some papers on his desk, dismissing me.

Now completely broke we went to the employment office and its odor of failed and decomposing humanity. The place was depressing past anyone's expectations. We were hurting for nicotine when a tubercular-looking man sat down and rolled a cigarette, licking it thoroughly to wet down the seam. Just as he lit up his name was called and he dropped it into a nearby bucket of sand. I picked up his creation and flicked off the sand.

You're not thinking seriously about smoking that, whispered UD. I whispered back that I was and put the butt to my lips. What the fuck, he said out loud, give me a drag. We sat there for three hours, but our names were never called.

That night we slept at Katie's again, and the next morning a bearded guy in his mid-twenties approached us on the dock and asked if we were the ones looking for passage to the States. If we were he had something for us. We followed him to a section of the harbor where the big boats tied up and signed onto *Eroica*, Enzo Ferrari's bright red seventy-foot yacht, as workaways. The vessel was just leaving the pier without a charter as we got there. It was 1330 hours on a Sunday. I remember because during the voyage to Florida I kept a journal in one of those marbled black and white composition books that everyone used in school. UD had given it to me for this purpose knowing he would never use it. I recently found it among my old papers with UD's real name inscribed on the inside front cover. Except for my entries the pages are blank.

The journal states that we came even with Sail Rock by 1800 hours averaging only 3.5 knots because the surrounding islands shielded us from the wind. UD and I cooked supper for the crew. There was a gas leak in the galley, and I became seasick. The entry continues:

> Charlotte Amalie presented a magnificent view from just outside the harbor, standing with the mid-aft sun beating down on her Danish roofs, but the islands on the horizon seemed

more intriguing, purple and misty; far ahead and to port—St. John . . . and by nightfall we could see the lights of Puerto Rico.

The sea so far has been fairly calm, and we are running with it and the wind; there is no cross-grained choppiness. The Caribbean from daybreak to sunset is always a deep purple. If I had first seen this ocean, I believe I would have named it the Indigo Sea. I have never seen anything so beautiful, and I doubt that even the dye the ancient Phoenicians produced could match it. . . . The sunset is beyond description. Since there is no longer any land in sight, the clouds seem even with our masts. Far to port the sun is now setting. The colors are silver and pale orange, and everything around has an icy-blue stillness to it.

In this entry I recalled two days from first grade when my family lived on Indian Creek Road. They were rare days when the whole sky was crimson. I had asked Mama to please give me those days so I would always have them, and she consented. Now I wanted every dawn and sunset for my own, to call up from memory if ever I was lonely. I wrote this at age nineteen aboard *Eroica*.

UD and I had been assigned to sleep in the forecastle. It was small, cramped, unventilated, hot, and access was by a deck hatch. The odor of bilge was overpowering. There were no bunks or blankets, just the bare boards. That first night we slept on deck, wrapped in a spare storm jib, looking up at the starry night and watching Orion hunt on his side. UD counted thirteen falling stars. It was his birthday; he had turned twenty-two.

Luminescent microorganisms lit up the sea where our passing broke apart its surface. At night the graceful balloon jib seemed almost like the creamy-white leg of a woman, the rest of her nestled among folds of a dark blanket and sprinkled over with diamonds. *Eroica* herself had the feminine qualities of beauty and grace.

The next morning after washing the breakfast dishes I carried the pan of dirty dishwater topside and was about to throw it overboard when the jib line lashed up, knocking the pan out of my hands and over my shoulder. Unfortunately the captain was at the helm and got it full in the face. I could tell he was pissed but all he said was, Dammit boy, I hope you learned something.

There were eight of us aboard. James Green was captain. Dave, who found us at the docks, was mate. Alexander, a wiry Corsican of forty-eight, served as navigator. He had twenty-nine years of sailing experience all over the world but was now married to an American woman and lived in Florida. He once yelled at me to beware of the boom. Later he explained in poor English that his best friend had been knocked overboard by a boom and lost. Tom, twenty-seven, was from Oregon. He'd been working at St. Thomas a year and decided to try Florida. There was Phil from Alabama who kept reminding me that if any of these goddamn Yankees started anything he and I might have to kick all their asses. He carried himself as if waiting for some large event.

Then there was the Colonel, the Captain's buddy, whose name I never knew. I don't think anyone knew it except Captain Green. The Colonel was retired Army, a World War II vet and hardcore alcoholic whose skin and hair looked newly unearthed at Arlington. The Colonel's drinking schedule went roughly as follows: 0700 to noon—beer; noon to 1430—martinis; 1430 to 1800—gin and tonics; 1800 until passing out—martinis again or rum and water. His shakes were so severe he could barely light his own Pall Malls. The Captain was also a lush, and it was Dave who kept things together. One of UD's and my morning duties was opening the Colonel's first beer and filling the Captain's cup with whiskey topped off with black coffee.

Some of my journal entries are so naïve I laugh out loud. The youthful lover of poetry reciting John Masefield's "Sea Fever" from memory and commenting how I pity the poor landlocked suckers who read it and yawn. What could they know? Yes, what, compared with an ancient nineteen-year-old seadog like myself. I wrote how I felt "so minute and close to nature, the Universe; I feel alienated and a part of it at the same time—something wonderful, sad, indescribable." Such awful writing helps explain why I became a scientist.

I noted that we were now in the Mona Passage, that the wind had increased, the swells grown larger; that we sighted a freighter off the port bow at 1000 hours moving southeast and away from us. I wrote that at 2100 hours the wind shifted from southwest to southeast and UD, Alex, Tom, and I mustered to reposition the balloon jib. We had been becalmed all day, averaging 1.5 knots. For supper UD and I cooked steak, rice, and beans, and UD commented that this sure as hell beat the jelly sandwiches at Mencho's Bakery in Christiansted.

Dave shaved off his beard and where before he looked nautical and wise he now looked goofy in the untanned face. Grow the beard again, the women will love you more, I advised.

Think so? Shit, I just shaved it off, but okay.

UD, Dave, Tom, and I swam in the afternoon, diving off the deck and climbing back up the rope ladder. Phil kept watch for sharks. The water was three miles deep; no telling what was swimming around deciding to feed at the surface.

We were almost totally becalmed. The boat was under full sail, yet I could swim faster than it was moving. In the morning I had noticed a small bird fluttering here and there, obviously tired and weak, but the luffing sails keep scaring it away. Finally it landed atop one of the masts and stayed. While we swam the Captain and Colonel sat in the shade drinking steadily and arguing incoherently about something. I later pointed out the bird, but they ignored me.

The wind picked up in the afternoon of day 4, although not enough to call for the mainsail. The air was stifling and still, the sea rolling gently. The lack of wind had delayed our estimated arrival time, so UD and I took inventory of the ship's stores. There was plenty of food but we recommended conserving water. From now on the dishes and laundry would be washed in seawater. No more freshwater showers either. In the morning I lost the garbage can while washing it out over the side. The handle snapped off and away it went. Earlier a school of dolphins swam past so close their breathing was audible. The skipper and Colonel had drunk the rum and gin aboard and ransacked the staterooms for what they could find. The Colonel broke his routine at breakfast when he and the Captain finished off the last drops of rum with their coffee. I gathered the night's collection of flying fishes from the deck. UD and I fried them and served them with eggs instead of bacon. The change was well received.

The previous evening when Alex decided to take over the cooking he became unbearable, slamming around the galley and swearing in French, finally telling UD and me to get the hell out. Here my journal entry reads, "Every damned Frenchman I've ever met has been [arrogant], and I can't decide whether or not to stereotype them." His stew was good but very spicy.

The next day the wind picked up and we averaged 7.5 knots for several hours, then it died and the boat sat rocking in the swells. A storm hit at suppertime, and everything in the galley rolled around as if suddenly given life. The forecastle was unbearably hot, the deck too wet for sleeping. In the cabin before supper Alex bent our ears about Corsica, the Colonel interrupting several times and advising me to attend West Point or at least join the Army. It would make a man of me, he said, his hands shaking violently.

Just after supper on day 7 the wind and rain came, and we went on deck to raise the balloon jib. The night was black and starless, the deck slippery and pitching violently. The Colonel and I were doing the hoisting. He was drunk and nearly went over the side, but I grabbed his arm in time and pulled him back, dropping the line to do so. The sail plunged down and Dave yelled, What the hell's going on? What are you guys doing over there?

UD and I ran out of cigarettes, and UD said it was maybe the first time in his life since age fourteen when another smoke was not available at least potentially. At dawn the next day we passed the island of San Salvador, its beacon blinking weakly at ten-second intervals. At 1800 hours the generator conked out, meaning no electricity or water for the remainder of the voyage—three days if Alex's projections held. There was still lots of beer. We ate and wrote by candlelight. Luckily the stove used propane. Alex was in a foul mood, screaming at everyone.

At 0715 hours on the ninth day we passed Abaco to starboard and entered the Hole in the Wall Passage. The wind rose, the sea rolling behind us in swells of eight feet or so. Captain Green mulled flying the spinnaker but decided not to. We ran out of candles, and water supplies became very low. Even coffee was banned.

I washed my shirts in seawater and hung them on the rail to dry. They were a gift from an older Cruzan woman on St. Croix. I knew her only to say hello on the street, but one day she stopped me and said how nice it was for a white man to treat her so politely. Afterward we always chatted a few minutes. I told her I was leaving for St. Thomas. I knew her son had been killed in the Korean War, and the next day she appeared carrying a suitcase filled with his clothes. We said goodbye on Hospital Street, and she was crying. She reached into her purse and carefully extracted a battered Bible. I want you to have this too, she said, and may the Lord always look after you. She patted my cheek and turned away. I gave the clothes I was unable to wear to a St. Thomas taxi driver in lieu of payment, but most of them I kept and wore.

We passed small islands belonging to millionaires, and through the glasses saw their mansions. At 1620 hours we entered on the Great Bahama Bank where the sea changed from indigo to light green; in some places the bottom was visible. UD and I had a fishing line out, and at 1700 hours we dragged a wahoo aboard that everyone agreed was at least a hundred pounds and six feet long. A half-hour later I hooked a five-foot barracuda and landed it alone. That night we ate wahoo steaks.

The next morning, the tenth day, we caught a male dorado weighing about thirty pounds. Alex cleaned and fried it. The flesh was firm and heavy, the best-tasting fish of my life. At 1300 hours the skyscrapers of Miami appeared, tall and purple in the distance. That night we came into Pier 66 but were ordered by Customs to remain aboard.

Just after breakfast the inspectors discovered hundreds of gallons of bootleg Scotch and vodka in five-gallon jerry cans secreted in the hold, and the crew was retained for questioning. Customs agents interviewed us all, but in the end only the Captain and Colonel were charged with smuggling, and late that afternoon the rest of us were released. The crew chipped in giving UD and me ten dollars each so we could buy cigarettes and food. We shook hands all around and wished each other fair winds. UD and I found a place near the docks that advertised all you could eat for three bucks.

In reading my journal for the first time after forty-six years, one thing stands out: a love of literature and desire to be a writer. The writerly part is dogged by doubt, specifically whether I had the talent or anything useful to say. What I didn't realize is that nineteen-year-olds rarely show evidence of talent or know anything worth listening to.

I could have brushed these worries aside and pushed on, but I didn't. The journal entries say nothing about why I decided simply to abandon writing for science—what prompted this decision, whether it was difficult. Perhaps it was relief knowing how much more straightforward science would be, how much less of me would be required. The two disciplines have similarities, however vague. The writer is confronted by a dictionary containing all the words he will ever need. His job is to string them together in special ways that test the rigor and intricacies of literature as art. The scientist, armed with nature's so-called laws and their appendices, devises hypotheses to probe the rough hides of theories. But there it ends. I evidently believed then that you can only *be* a writer, but you can *become* a scientist. And so I took the less risky path and became one.

UD and I discussed working in Florida for travel money, but I was now committed to biology and needed to get back in school. The writing was too slow in coming, perhaps because I was low on experiences and ideas, not to mention suffering, although when I finally did get home my weight was only one hundred thirty-five pounds. UD decided to head for New York City and work the winter there, and in late spring we would meet Cap at Beach Haven.

I telephoned Daddy who agreed to send us bus fare, and we bought tickets to Huntington, West Virginia. Once there UD hung out a few days before heading north. The night before he left some of my college buddies bought us each at trip upstairs at a local whorehouse as welcome home and going away gifts. This hospitality impressed UD greatly, and he said he would always feel kindly toward West Virginians.

9

*I*n Witold Gombrowicz's novel *Pornografia* the protagonist realizes that a murderer is distinguished by a decision to smell the flowers with his spirit instead of his nose. Surely this is worth discussing, but doing so would have been unlikely among my classmates or acquaintances at the university. In fact there was no talk about anything worthwhile I can remember. This was especially disconcerting during the freshman year when I dabbled in the humanities. The students seemed to care only about grades.

I kept my mouth shut and went along. What the hell, I figured, thinking in abstract terms is probably irrelevant to real life. During free time in bars or the student union we talked about beer, pussy, and sports, never anything remotely intellectual, and getting drunk and laid (preferably after a football game) were the only activities worth pursuing.

My classmates seemed nervous around concepts, fearing the abstract as if it might suddenly turn vicious. Instead they embraced a flippant nonchalance toward knowledge, joking about learning and purposely mispronouncing terms. It was smartass hillbilly stuff, and I knew this because no one I had met at the beach tried to seem purposely ignorant.

On campus, for example, was a kid from Canada named François. Always wary of the foreigner the guys would say to him, Hey Franz-*wah*, how're they hanging? Still think you're in Kwee-*beck*? And then someone would wonder aloud, Where the fuck is Kwee-*beck* anyhow? Eventually they simply called him Frankie because it seemed less dangerous than changing something in themselves.

And about the girls: how'd it go last night, W.D., shoot any beaver?

Hail yeah, shot one off'n a barstool. A man cain't shoot beaver and not eat it. Makes for poor conservation practice, har, har.

The objective was to stay good ol' boys at all costs, damn urbanity, and full speed ahead. Sophistication led only to ostracism, and no way in hell did Greek mythology or art history help you land a good job after college. Leave that stuff to the queers up in New York. The mantra was just learn what you need to know, ignore the rest, and drink a beer. The problem is, at that age everyone is too stupid to realize which branches of knowledge really are necessary or might at least make your future more enlightened.

*I*t came as no surprise that little changed after I returned from St. Croix and switched to the sciences. There was natural selection and evolution to learn about, the spin of electrons through their orbits, the practicalities of laboratory techniques and solving equations, and all of it together required far more time than the humanities but proportionately less imagination. A certain satisfaction accompanied finishing a math or chemistry problem, although this feeling paled next to deciphering a poem's artfulness or examining the brush strokes of a painting in changing light. In fact the two were nothing alike and only a burning interest in natural history kept me from quitting school altogether. The memorization was brutal, the labs a drudgery. I thought it would never end, but of course it did, and leaving the university after completing all requirements was like getting out of jail. I vowed never to return, although later I enrolled at another university and earned a doctorate in biology.

During that semester after the Caribbean I felt increasingly disaffected, like a movie actor whose words and lips are out of sync. It seemed I could step back and see myself talking and gesturing while everyone smiled hesitantly and looked away. I recognized later what it was, merely a brightening realization of how inept language and gesture transmit thought, and how much they lie. Ants following a scent trail are more efficient and honest.

On Friday nights I usually got loaded and blacked out, not remembering how or when I got home. Strangely, no one seemed to notice, further evidence of how futile the human capacity to communicate really is. Twice I queried friends about my behavior the previous weekend. Had I killed anyone? I wondered silently. Which acquaintances and friends had I offended? You were there, they said, and you didn't seem that blasted. In fact, they added, you appeared downright normal, for you, quieter maybe and not so much of an asshole, but don't ask us, we were drunk.

My grades started to drop, and I slipped into a dark depression devoid of any self-pity. Nothing seemed worthwhile, the future holding only boredom and dissatisfaction. Outwardly I was my standard self: friendly but not excessively so, sardonic, unkempt, a cigarette usually stuck in my face.

The nights when I didn't black out were tormented by recurrent dreams of floating down a stygian river past deserted towns and villages. How I might have escaped to the shore is uncertain because it was never clear whether I was swimming or drifting aboard a raft or boat. No memory remains of even trying. I recall a sense of agitation, expectation maybe, for a gull or some other living thing to appear and keep me company, but there was nothing: no sound, no movement except a liquid sensation of water that felt neither cold nor warm. The light was bleak as if filtered through high clouds, the obsidian wavelets hard and sharp, reflective as facets in a coal seam. The river seemed intent on dragging me to the bottom, on merging its melanic pigment with my black mood.

I struggled languidly, apathetically, and the river stroked me with its silky wetness, writhed over my skin like a serpent. Prolong this another night, it seemed to say, thrash around if you wish, although it isn't I who shall drown you in the end but your own impoverished creativity, the capacity to soar. You relinquished art for paint-by-the-numbers, metered lines for instruction manuals. Go ahead, practice those exacting descriptions of nature. Art in all its forms shows us what *can't* be described. Poor ignorant bastard, now you'll never know. Remember me when the weight of illusion tugs at your ankles and pulls your nose under. Think of me when that final light explodes across your brain in angstrom units instead of shadow play.

The cloud lifted so gradually, so imperceptibly, that I barely noticed. The level of alienation stayed about the same, but the depression lessened until I could drink and remain conscious, sleep without dreaming of a black river, and finally break free from the notion of being a writer.

*T*hat same semester we were doing fieldwork in a couple of the biology classes, the naturalists having at last parted company with the premed geeks. That had been a relief. The premed majors came to class in jackets and ties ready to fight to the death for a good grade while we biologists stood apart from the fray, amused, not really caring what our scores were. We were now keeping company with true believers, professors who understood natural processes.

One of these was Professor Fromm, a tall lanky Southerner with flowing white hair, matching goatee, and a waxed handlebar moustache stained tan by nicotine. The other professors wore jackets to class, but Professor Fromm strode the halls dressed in a dark suit and string tie. Mammals were his specialty, bats in particular, and when he talked about them—their infinite variety and beauty—he smiled like someone high on heavy sensation. Professor Fromm walked with an uneven stride while looking at the ground near his feet, as if stepping along a series of railroad ties. Another student once speculated that it came from always watching for voles and other small cryptic mammals.

On a spring evening he and I gathered up the field gear, loaded it into one of the department's battered pickups, drove across the bridge to Kentucky, and parked in a field. It was one of those shimmering evenings thick with fireflies and whippoorwill calls but otherwise so quiet you could hear mice scrabbling through last year's leaves. We walked to a darkening tree line where three of the locals were fishing on the bank of a slow creek. They had their worms and cane poles and bobbers. Aquatic insects, newly emerged, dimpled the eddies, and bream were rising to them with soft sucking sounds. The creek looked slick and silvery in the fading light, black where it hunkered under the overhanging trees.

My young friend and I are from over at the university, Professor Fromm announced. He wants to seine up some fish downstream of here. It shouldn't hurt your fishing any. And while he's doing that would you mind if I shot a few bats?

Um, no, I reckon not, they said, slightly bewildered. You a drinking man?

As it happens I am, the professor replied. He squatted beside them and twirled one handlebar of his moustache. There was some shifting around as they passed him the bottle of bourbon. He took a swallow before handing it my way. Now that's awfully charitable of you, said Professor Fromm. He stood and wiped his mouth on his sleeve, gave a polite nod, and strode into the twilight to shoot some bats.

That semester I hung out occasionally with a psychology major named Felix who lived in a second-floor tenement flat. His roomie was a white Peking duck trained to use kitty litter. Felix called it his "watch duck" because when anyone knocked on the door it quacked furiously and beat its tiny wings. Felix was slovenly with a pasty complexion and one of those physiques on whom a belt looks more like the middle band of a barrel. His place always smelled like a pond.

Felix was still a virgin but not from lack of trying. He was heavily into the study of pheromones and figured that if humans produced any they would be associated with sex. His hope was to attract a woman chemically, the odor of his manhood rendering her instantly limp and wet as if stunned by a hammer or overly hard penis. Every Wednesday the nursing school held a smoker, and several of us went regularly. Felix often came along after first jerking off in his necktie and then swiping it around his genitals.

Tonight's the night, he'd whisper excitedly, smelling faintly of distressed sperm and pond ooze and trailing bits of pinfeathers as we pushed through the doors.

Of course it never worked.

Judie came down on the train from New York to visit in the spring of 1963 and called later saying she was pregnant. She was enrolled in a one-year program at the Katharine Gibbs School, a prestigious training ground for executive secretaries in Manhattan. After she finished classes in May we got married and moved into a dingy apartment across from the campus. I worked taking care of the biology department's greenhouse and also found a night job as janitor at a bowling alley.

I'd met Judie at the beach the summer before, eighteen and just out of high school, a rangy brunette of notable leg. She and her friends stayed at the Evelyn House and thumbed to and from work at an A&W root beer stand in Beach Haven. After Labor Day when the Evelyn House closed Judie, Cap, UD, and I cleared out the cobwebs underneath the porch and camped there several nights. A buddy from college, Todd Case, who had come up from West Virginia by bus for the end of the season, was with us too.

There had been a party at Holgate the night before Labor Day, and a guy I barely knew drove his beat forty-nine Ford flathead-eight out onto the beach. During the party the tide came in, submerging it up to the engine block and sticking it fast in the sand. The next day we got the township maintenance crew to bring down a tow truck. Originally black, the old Ford now had no finish at all. Neither did it have a roof, the convertible top having long since rotted off. The front seat was gone, and so was the windshield. Miraculously it started when its owner turned the key, and the engine ran so quietly you scarcely heard a sound.

I'll give you thirty-five bucks, I told the guy, which was most of my money. He said we had a deal.

There was no time to write away to West Virginia for a registration and license plate. We had Todd's return bus fare to buy gas. For seats we stole two empty beer kegs from behind Buckalew's, wedged them in place with cinder blocks and bricks, and set off south driving mostly after dark to avoid the police.

I kept the car a couple of years and all it ever needed was gas and the occasional oil change. With the arrival of cold weather that autumn I took it to a junkyard and bought a roof and windshield from a wrecked 1950 Ford hard top. They fit onto the body well enough. I bolted the roof to the frame and inserted the windshield using what remained of the original molding. Bent coat hangers served as spacers, and the voids were filled with bathtub caulking. A front seat came from another wreck. In the time remaining before graduation Judie, our daughter Sara, and I even drove to New Jersey to visit her family, the only discomfort being the lack of a workable heater and two flat tires along the way.

10

After my final class in January 1965 Judie, Sara, Judie's dog, and I drove to Niagara Falls in a crappy fifty-eight Chevy. A public aquarium was under construction, and I had been hired with my new bachelor's degree as an aquarist at a hundred dollars a week. The organization was putting us up in a motel south of town on Buffalo Avenue until we could find an apartment. The city was gray, the air ripe with effluents excreted by chemical plants lining the American side of the Niagara River. Overnight it snowed, and when I looked out the window the following morning the cars in the lot were silent humped camels on a white desert.

For shoes I owned a ragged pair of sneakers, which I pulled on over yesterday's socks, then jeans, a wool shirt, and a jacket, and trudged out to a nearby diner. I got breakfast for all of us, a newspaper so Judie could check the apartment listings, and returned to the room. After eating I borrowed a snow shovel from the motel manager, shoveled out the car, drove to an office the aquarium had rented across the street from the construction site, and began studying the blueprints. The aquarium was only a large frozen hole surrounded by construction machinery.

Judie found us a rental in a former World War II military barracks in the north end of town. The apartments were decrepit and sliding rapidly to tenement status, but they had two floors and were all we could afford on my salary. We moved in our few belongings and bought some secondhand furniture. The next-door neighbors were Grace and Ronnie, who sometimes expressed their feelings by hurling objects that ricocheted off the common wall of our living rooms. From over on our side even the radio turned to full volume wasn't decent competition.

Grace was maybe ten years older than Ronnie, although her actual age was hard to assess. She lived mostly in her nightgown and had the look of someone held against cold trap rock and serially abused by rejected sperm donors. Ronnie was chubby and balding and liked his beer. He worked at one of the plants along the river and avoided coming home when he could. Ronnie yelled Fucking asshole! a lot, and it was often hard to tell from our side if he was addressing Grace or some character on the teevee.

The aquarium director was Winfield Brady, a short blocky guy of forty-five and very tough. He once held the world underwater swimming record. Five years earlier he had entered the big exhibit aquarium at Gulfarium in Fort Walton Beach, Florida, wearing scuba gear and a primitive wetsuit and swum in a circle for many hours, stopping only to exchange scuba tanks underwater or accept a soggy candy bar from another diver. He finally surfaced when his legs cramped so completely he could no longer move them and he was shaking and turning blue from hypothermia. I forget now the number of miles he actually swam or whether straightened out they might have stretched halfway to Pensacola. Win's brush cut and ice-gray eyes gave him the stern look of a military man in civilian clothes, but he was a terrific boss and knew lots about the marine sciences.

I was working long hours, and Judie resented it. You should tell Win you have a family, she said.

Win's there working with us, and he has a family too, I explained. Everyone is humping so we can open before summer. Tell him you aren't going to work nights anymore, she said.

Then you better find a job, I told her, because I won't have one. At these times families have to sacrifice. Judie didn't understand this, although later in life she herself became a workaholic. The problem was obvious, and I was too immature and focused to see it clearly. We were in a new city without friends or family support. It was winter, the weather was brutal, and Judie was confined indoors for long periods with only a little kid and a dog for company. I should have shown more sympathy.

After we had been working a month or so Win held a meeting with me, the other two aquarists (both named Charlie), and George Webster, who was in charge of maintenance. Boys, he said, it's assholes and elbows from here on. No more days off. We need to open this place by summer to start making money and pay off the debt.

So we worked harder, which pissed off our wives even more. Charlie Beck had figured out a procedure for reproducing artifacts resembling corals, rocks, and logs in fiberglass, and set up a workshop to begin casting them. Charlie Radcliffe and I were helping George construct holding tanks from marine plywood and glass, making lists of animals we needed, and participating in design and content of the exhibits with Win and Charlie Beck. The days and nights merged, and we went home only to eat and sleep a few hours.

Progress was rapid, and by April the building was up and the aquarium tanks were in place with the plumbing installed. Ours would be the first public aquarium that relied entirely on artificial seawater rather than water taken directly from the ocean. We mixed it in subterranean vats holding ten thousand gallons using a formula based on an early version of Instant Ocean®. From there the water could be pumped upstairs to the exhibits.

Charlie Beck was installing his artifacts and arranging them strategically into naturalistic settings depicting coral reefs, Pacific coast kelp beds, North American lakes, South American tropical rivers, Southeast Asian swamps, and so forth. Some of the largest and most spectacular displays would feature coral reef fishes and invertebrates. We started ordering in freshwater exotics and the California specimens from dealers around the country and acclimating them to the holding tanks, but Win planned on collecting the coral reef animals himself. He and I were the only staff members who could scuba dive, so I would be assisting him.

The aquarium owned a new flat-nosed van, metallic blue with our logo—three leaping dolphins—painted on the side. Inside were two seats separated by the engine cover, and the rest was space without windows so no one could look in and see what you were carrying. We stuffed it with scuba equipment, nets, fish traps made in our shop under Win's direction, and tools for building holding pens for the coral fishes and invertebrates we planned to catch in the Florida Keys. George built a roof container out of plywood for additional storage and painted it blue like the truck.

I would drive the van to Destin on Florida's west coast where a friend of Win's named Buck Destin, a commercial pompano fisherman, was supposed to catch the dolphins. Win had hired Chuck Emmett, a Florida dolphin trainer, to train the animals and bring them north shortly before opening day. Win planned to fly down and meet me in Destin along with Jay Smith, nephew of Kelvin Smith, the Cleveland philanthropist who had financed the aquarium's construction. Jay was a six-foot-six hedonist who weighed maybe three hundred and fifty pounds. He told Win he knew how to scuba dive, wanted to help us collect fish, and would pay his own expenses. It seemed a harmless idea.

When I got to Destin I telephoned Buck as instructed to find where Win and Jay were staying. Buck advised trying the Blue Moon, a bar near the water. It was early afternoon when I found the place. I went inside and asked the bartender if he knew Win. Oh sure, the guy said, but he's not here right now. I asked where he was. He's in jail, the bartender said. He got in a fight last night right there, and he pointed to a stool next to where I was standing. The night bartender, he said, had to call the cops.

I got directions to the jail and went to see Win. He was sitting in a cell badly hung over, although no worse for the fight. Pay the fine and get me out, he ordered.

I called the aquarium from a pay phone outside and asked our accountant, a fastidious fairy whose mother shined his shoes and chose his necktie every morning, to wire me two hundred dollars. I need to know what it's for, he said sourly. I can't just send you money. How do I know you're not drinking and having a nice Florida vacation?

You don't, I replied, but send it anyway.

I need to write what it's for in my ledger, he said.

Then write bail money for the boss. And by the way, if it's not here in two hours the boss says to kiss your ass goodbye.

The money's on the way, he said, and I'm going to have a chat with Win about your tone when he gets back. I told him that Win was looking forward to it.

I went to Western Union and then sprung Win, who said he needed a drink, a few hairs from the canine, he said. Jay was late getting down but would meet us at the Blue Moon. Jay showed up shortly afterward, and we had seafood platters together at the bar. Around eight Buck came in and drank a beer with us. He was leaving to go pompano fishing. Win told me to go along and pick out four fairly small dolphins, two males and two females. I said I had never seen a dolphin up close, much less sexed one. Win sketched out the differences on a napkin and told me to take along the tape measure and keep them around seven feet. He and Jay would stay behind to drop off Jay's rental car and meet me early next morning at the dock. Meanwhile they planned to drink a little and maybe rustle some cracker pussy off the barstools.

What I knew about dolphins came from reading, mainly a book published in 1961 by John C. Lilly titled *Man and Dolphin*. Lilly had graduated from medical school in 1942, the year I was born, and soon became interested in comparative brain anatomy and the potential of interspecies communication. Lilly argued that humankind had better tackle the problem before we encounter aliens from space, at which point it might be too late. In looking around at likely candidates here on Earth he hit on the dolphin because its brain-to-body-mass ratio was close to that of humans.

Lilly, a self-professed man of kindness and peace, arranged with Marine Studios in St. Augustine, Florida, to conduct experiments using some of the extra bottlenose dolphins. He removed them from the water and strapped them to tables, often for days at a time, while probes were inserted into their brains. On discovering the loci of pleasure and pain he trained them to push levers either to lessen the agony or continue the good feelings. Naturally the animals died, but there were always more. Meanwhile he recorded the sounds they made as the electrical current was raised or lowered, detected evidence of mimicry, and decided that the best approach at communication would be to teach them English. He interpreted certain behaviors of captive dolphins in Marineland's big oceanarium as evidence of high intelligence and altruism. Evidently he was the only witness at some of these events because no one has seen them since. Lilly concluded that here was an alien intelligence perhaps superior to our own, one in which legends and other aspects of advanced culture were passed down through generations.

So was born the myth of the mystical dolphin, custom-made for the sixties when Eastern religious teachings and mysticism of all sorts entered the hippie mainstream. Life seemed better out there in the blue ocean where nothing—not even gravity—interfered with the capacity of sentient animals such as dolphins to contemplate the Universe and perfect tales that might relegate *Beowulf* to comic-book status. These beliefs were often reinforced by drugs—LSD in particular—which made the world turn funny colors and induced dreams that its users interpreted as communication on a higher plane. In my personal experience this is simply your id's hairy paw swatting at the lowest rung of consciousness, intermittently grabbing and letting go, although generally not until after you puked.

Lilly wrote about dissecting out the brain of a beached pilot whale in Maine. The animal had been dead a while, and the stench alone was sufficient to repel curious onlookers. According to Lilly it measured twenty-eight feet, or about eight feet longer than some of the biggest specimens ever recorded. Lilly also wrote that after a day of hacking through putrid blubber and bone he and his colleagues stuffed their clothes into the trunk of the car and drove back to Massachusetts. By the time they arrived the odor had dissipated completely.

Had he really been there? In later years I helped dissect many dead whales and dolphins, realizing immediately that my clothes were best discarded someplace far away. Dead cetaceans have a heavy cloying odor and a greasy consistency that penetrates and coats everything you touch. After one of these episodes our dogs would bound up to sniff my colleagues and me with new appreciation and try vainly to roll on us where we stood. Wives and girlfriends, emitting involuntary retching sounds, ran the other way flapping their hands in front of their faces. You can't get around it: a dead whale smells worse than just about anything.

I suspected Lilly of smoking some fine dope, but that aside most of what I knew about dolphins had come from his book. Win was no help. To him dolphins were simple objects of entertainment, scarcely worthy of comment. As a marine biologist he knew all about their mammalian status, but this didn't stop him from calling them "fish," which he meant as a slap at Lilly's curiously sterile hagiography.

I ransacked the reading memory for useful bits of information, feeling slow panic when nothing surfaced. Buck and his crew of two set the seine along the beach in water so thin the boat bumped across the bottom, sticking sometimes and wallowing like a hog before wrenching free. The sea-end of the seine was then pulled toward the beach, and the crew and I jumped overboard.

The water was shallow enough to stand. Usually there were lots of pompano and occasionally dolphins, which Buck said were there to eat the fish. We released the bigger dolphins first by lowering a section of float line and pushing them over it. They were heavy and slippery as wet rubber, and sometimes they fought furiously. Afterward the net was pulled in until everything was beached and I could look over the remaining animals using a flashlight. We lifted likely candidates aboard on stretchers and laid them on their sides on foam pads so I could measure and sex them and look for any lesions or other defects. While I did this Buck and the crew released the rest and tossed the pompano onto ice in the hold. We set and pulled the net at intervals all night. Eventually I had four keeper animals on the aft deck and was wetting them intermittently with a deck hose.

We arrived at the dock about five in the morning, but Win and Jay weren't there. I gave the crew some money and asked them to rig a canvas over the dolphins but not directly on top of them, and to keep them wet when they could take time from unloading fish. Buck and I got in his pickup and went to the Blue Moon, figuring it was a surer bet than the motel.

They're not here, said the bartender.

But the van is still in the parking lot, I pointed out.

They got drunk and rowdy, the bartender continued, so I called the cops, and the cops drove them home. They're at some motel. Another guy was with them, a guy I've seen around before.

I had a key to the van, so with Buck leading the way in his pickup we went to their motel room and pounded on the door. Oh good Christ, Win said when he opened it, do I feel awful.

Jay lifted an eyelid from the other bed and looked at me. You prick, he said.

The third guy was Chuck Emmett, the trainer, who was sleeping in his car just outside. We unloaded the van, stacking everything in the motel room, then all of us went to the dock, put two dolphins on foam pads behind the seats and the two others on foam in Buck's pickup, and took them to a saltwater swimming pool at a rundown motel where Win had made temporary arrangements. Chuck was to stay there in a room fronting the pool and in a day or two transfer the animals to Gulfarium in Fort Walton Beach where their training would commence.

Chuck was a wiry worn-down cracker of maybe forty with sad eyes, slumped shoulders, and a face like an explanation of gravity. He was an alcoholic, but Win had known him for years and insisted that if you overlooked some of the binge drinking, Chuck was more reliable than most drunks. Years later, when I visited Win after he retired in the Florida Keys, he told me Chuck had telephoned collect one stormy night from Miami, drunk and nearly incoherent, saying he had met a Bahamian girl and was leaving for Nassau. He said he had a borrowed twelve-foot skiff with a fifteen-horse outboard and maybe enough gas, and then hung up. Chuck couldn't swim and knew nothing about navigation. Win never heard from him again.

Chuck left to buy fish for the dolphins from a seafood wholesaler, and the rest of us went to the Blue Moon for hamburgers and beers. Late that afternoon we left for the Keys. I needed sleep and wedged myself among the piles of gear in back and dropped off. We stopped at a diner around sunset where Jay bought three quarts of bourbon at a liquor store across the road. After supper we changed drivers and started passing a bottle and by two or so the next morning with Win driving, Jay in the passenger seat, and me sitting between them on the engine cover, Win took a corner too fast and flipped the van three times, crushing it like a beer can. My left leg went through the windshield, cutting a deep semicircular gash across the front above the ankle.

We have to sterilize that, Win said. Inside the wreck he found a bottle of bourbon that was mostly full and poured some on my cut.

Jesus Christ! Jay screamed. Don't waste that on his goddamn leg. He yanked the bottle out of Win's hand and took a rough swig. There were no first aid supplies so I used strips from my shirt as a makeshift bandage. The bleeding stopped, replaced by persistent throbbing. No cars came along. We sat in the road finishing the bottle under hardscrabble moonlight feeling like spare parts.

No one had much to say. The van reflected weakly from where it nestled in scrub off to the side. There were owls and whippoorwills somewhere around and a big puddle of oil next to us glistening like new asphalt. Jay told about meeting the woman who was now his wife just after such a wreck. He had been trying to beat a train at a railroad crossing one night and nearly made it. She was a candy striper at the Cleveland Clinic, and she bounced into the room making the glorious noises women make around babies and puppies of an age when both still shit themselves. Thinking he was helpless too she got close and Jay reached out and stuck his hand underneath her dress. Now I wish I'd broken that arm too, he said.

Eventually a state policeman arrived. He drove us to a motel and ordered the van lifted out of the sand and palmettos onto a flatbed truck and dropped at a junkyard. The next morning my leg was swollen and hurting. The cut itself had turned black, the surrounding area dark red. The motel owner drove me to a clinic under a stand of large pines where a duty doctor cleaned the wound, applied twenty stitches, and issued antibiotics, and when I got back we called a taxi and went to see the van. Although the roof rack had been smashed, the nets inside appeared to be undamaged. In fact, most of the gear had survived except a scuba tank that had jetted around some after its valve snapped off.

After inspecting the damage Win said, Shit, now what?

We buy a new van, said Jay, who was a millionaire many times over, and he bought one at a Chevy dealer using his credit card. The paperwork took the rest of the day, and when we left the next morning Win ordered everyone to stay sober until we reached Islamorada in the Keys. We were to stay with Jimmy Crovetti, one of his pals from Philadelphia who was living in a rented house fronted by a canal where we could set up floating pens. Crovetti, a South Philly hood and semi-retired car thief, was cooling his heels in the Keys until things settled down up north. Specifically which things he declined to mention, at least to me, and I never asked.

I was supposed to keep my leg dry for two weeks, but the first day in Islamorada I took a hand net and caught some colorful shrimps by wading along a shallow part of the canal wall. Later we went to a hardware store and bought chicken wire and hardware cloth, lengths of two-by-twos, blocks of Styrofoam, and other supplies for constructing the pens. Win told me the dimensions to make them and he and Jay left for Miami in the empty van. I worked that day and into the evening building three large pens. The next morning I hung dive weights off the bottoms for stability, put blocks of Styrofoam around the tops, and set them afloat in the canal. I also baited some of the fish traps and threw them in.

Win and Jay came back two days later with a couple of hookers they met in a bar. Jay had hired their services plus living expenses for three weeks. One was a lanky freckled girl with reddish hair, the other a short brunette going to pork. They were bubbly and seemed genuinely interested in what we were doing. Meanwhile the traps baited with bread and frozen ballyhoo had yielded several juvenile angelfishes, a large butterflyfish, a couple of triggerfishes, a few grunts, and some small spiny lobsters.

Crovetti owned a boat, and Win and I started making daily runs to the reef to collect. Jay and Crovetti stayed behind, saying someone had to guard the women. Small fishes were caught using hand nets, the large ones by dropping a short gill net across a bare spot in the reef and checking it every couple of hours. We also set anchored fish traps marked by floating buoys and made dives underneath bridges along the Overseas Highway during slack tides, collecting sea anemones and other invertebrates that inhabited crevices or clung to the bottom in the swift currents. In late afternoon we picked up the nets and traps and returned to the dock, the deck tank filled with fishes and other creatures. Diving continued day and night, and within a week our holding pens were full.

Win bought several dozen Styrofoam boxes with cardboard shipping cartons from a local fish collector in Islamorada, and we started rising at dawn to put the animals in plastic bags with some seawater and then into the boxes. Usually the girls made coffee and helped us. They decided that marine biology might be a good career move if they ever gave up whoring.

The tall one, who had taken to leafing through our field guides and was learning to identify some of the fishes, practiced her new knowledge while we filled the bags. One morning she said, This one's a juvenile gray angelfish, right?

No, it's a French angelfish because the tail spot is round, I answered.

Ah damn, she said disgustedly, I thought I had the little bastards pinned down. It's like a pimp convention where everybody looks the same. Later that week when Win and I were together on the boat I suggested hiring her to be an aquarist in Niagara Falls, but Win said that was probably a bad idea.

With the van loaded to the ceiling I would drive to Miami International and send the boxes air freight for Charlie or Charlie to meet at Buffalo International. From there it was a forty-five minute drive to the aquarium. Packing, shipping, and the round-trip drive took a whole day and had to be done three days a week for the next two weeks. Usually I drove, in which case Win took the boat to the reef and dived alone, but sometimes he went to the airport and left me instructions about where to go and what to collect.

One morning Win asked Jay to take the Miami run, but he laughed. He and Crovetti, naked except for Coppertone and carrying a box of cigars and a pitcher of screwdrivers, were on the way to the back yard to sunbathe with the girls. Crovetti was deeply tanned, but Jay resembled a bloated lobster newly finished in hot oil. He said he was thinking of leaving his wife and kids and moving in with Crovetti and the girls. The best thing in life, he said, is bought nooky, and in an ideal world you don't even need clothes, just a credit card, a liquor store across the street, and pizza delivery.

For the first couple of weeks Jay stayed behind when Win and I went collecting, but one morning as we looked over the tide tables preparing for a dive under a bridge he decided to come along. I need the exercise, he said, a man can't drink and fuck all the time.

We drove to the bridge and lugged everything down to the water. Jay opened his dive bag and wriggled into his custom wetsuit, donned flippers and mask, and asked for his scuba tank. Everything was new, freshly out of the box and top of the line. I lifted the tank onto his back, and he strapped it in place. Then he asked me to get out his new underwater camera and take his picture. This, he said, is evidence to show my wife I actually came here and didn't just check into a whorehouse in Miami for three weeks. I had barely tripped the shutter when he sat down on a large rock and started peeling everything off. He was grunting and sweating from the effort.

What are you doing? I asked.

You don't think I'm going in *there*, do you? He pointed at the water. Come and get me after you and Brady catch the fish. I'll be in that bar up next to the bridge where it's air conditioned. And bring my stuff, he added, I'm too goddamn hot to carry it.

That night Jay threw a party. He bought several quarts of grain alcohol and lots of different kinds of juices and mixed up batches of Jay's Jungle Juice in some of the Styrofoam shipping boxes. After adding ice he passed around paper cups. It was deadly stuff. The girls cranked the radio to full volume, and Crovetti started waving around a .22 caliber pistol saying it was sometimes the instrument of choice for mobster hit men and bragging about what a great shot he was.

Maybe, Jay said, but I'm better.

Horseshit, Crovetti answered. He handed the pistol to Jay and stepped across the room. If you're so good then shoot this bottle of rum out of my hand.

Jay took aim and fired two rounds in rapid succession, missing the bottle but blowing out a window and shooting Crovetti in the forearm. Crovetti crumpled to the floor howling. Maybe you're a better shot after all, Jay said, and helped himself to a cup of juice.

Win was laughing so hard he could scarcely breathe. Christ, Jay, that was pathetic, he said.

Crovetti's howls turned to whimpers, so Win and I drove him to the emergency room where the admitting nurse wanted to know what happened.

Someone shot him, I said.

I can tell that, replied the nurse. Who did it?

We don't know, Win said, but can you fix him so he quits whining?

He has a bullet wound, sir, said the nurse sternly, and you're all drunk, aren't you?

Yes ma'am, we surely are, Win said.

The wound turned out to be not very serious. They numbed Crovetti's arm and patched him up. After the police interviewed us and wrote a report we took Crovetti home where the girls fawned over him and promised to make him feel better.

We needed two big sea turtles for an exhibit. Back then, the sixties, it was still legal to catch and sell sea turtles for soup and peddle the lacquered carapaces as souvenirs. At the docks in Key West was a section called the Turtle Kraals that housed a cannery for producing turtle soup and a holding area for live turtles. I can't recall if the cannery was still open in April 1965, but the Kraals themselves were doing steady business.

Win, Jay, and I took the van to Key West one afternoon after a morning's drinking. Most of the animals had been captured and shipped, and we were basically finishing up. Jay bought some bourbon and a case of beer for the trip, and we arrived with bladders about to burst.

Pull into that mall, Jay said to me. I pulled in and parked, and Jay got out and started pissing against the car parked next to us. Spattering rain sounds on a sunny day, then potent runoff. Jay the wasted red giant left ripening too long in the sun and belching ineffectual decay.

Who the hell are you? he said around his cigar to the people who owned the car and were thinking about getting into it. They took offense and called the police. Win and I were pissing too, except on the pavement. A cop car stopped us just as we were leaving. We followed the cop to the police station and were fined for public urination.

At the Kraals we bought two green turtles, a male and female. You paid by the pound, and these weighed about a hundred pounds each. The fisherman who caught them, most likely a Bahamian, had turned them onto their backs and tied their front flippers together through holes made with a knife or screwdriver. Sea turtles can survive for weeks like that. We put them in the van and drove back to Islamorada. The next day Win and I built wooden crates so they could be shipped to Buffalo.

11

I've often wondered how much introspection and compassion are healthy before the mind starts to bubble uncontrollably. Compassion has been notably lacking in my character, a hand-me-down from the grim paternal side, while my mama's kin not only wallow in kindness but practice it like hillbilly Buddhists or Christians somehow regressed away from bigotry.

I started thinking along these lines after Judie and Sara left me among empty walls where the silence held reminders not just of disruption but a form of personal failure. All at once life was strange and depressing. Could I have done anything differently to change things? Probably not. Judie wanted the finer things and showed little inclination to wait until they might be earned. I missed Sara, and the experience was my first encounter with loneliness, the sensation of a hole in your being and no psychic tools around to fix it.

Loneliness, in a sense, is nothing but a special category of selfishness, the unrelieved sorries. Lonely people think mostly about themselves and very little about others. To most, I suppose, the cause of this grief would have been immediately obvious, but not to me, evidence of how a lifetime spent avoiding introspection can render your own problems mysterious, unique, and therefore revolutionary to all previous human experience. I recalled feeling occasional pity for others but never for myself, and certainly not for the larger notion of organic life. How could I as one paid to separate its ticking components? Or so I reasoned. In hindsight even birth is lonely unless we're twins; then we leap down the birth canal—down that tunnel of love—one behind the other, headfirst or breach, it hardly matters, and exit screaming at the bottom. No loneliness. Ever. From that first day on the waterslide.

I analyzed the situation for several weeks, sleepwalking through my duties at the aquarium, and arrived at three conclusions. First, no one else could repair the damage or even help to repair it. Talking it over with a friend would achieve nothing, change nothing. I would have conversations with myself instead, that inner being now trembling and confused, that maddest of existentialists.

Second, I needed to convince myself that the relationship with Judie was over and focus exclusively on Sara. She was now my family; Judie had voluntarily cut herself adrift. Third, my job needed to be more meaningful, and I could make it so by stretching its intellectual potential beyond previous boundaries. By focusing hard on biology and chemistry I would fill in the time. I resolved to read everything pertaining to my profession and try to understand it all, and then I would write a book. Writing would be a long-term project dedicated to those hours of the night when I was consumed by the high lonesomes. I didn't know much about technical writing, but I owned a typewriter.

I also needed to abandon the apartment and its memories. Judie had taken the car with her to New Jersey, and I couldn't afford to buy another. I found a one-room flat in downtown Niagara Falls a block from work. It had a Murphy bed in the wall, a kitchenette, two windows looking onto the street, and a tiny bathroom. I lived there a year before renting a one-bedroom apartment in the same building, which allotted space for a large desk that my brother-in-law John and I lugged up three flights of narrow stairs one hot summer day when he and Jane were visiting. Later I found that it came apart easily and I could have moved it alone in pieces. John never forgave me.

The apartment was on the corner of Third and Main across the street from Guarino's Italian Restaurant. Gordy Guarino managed the family business while his parents, Italian immigrants, cooked in the kitchen. Gordy was a heart attack on call, an overweight chain smoker who sweated every detail. He and his wife had six kids, and Gordy was always on the phone shouting at her about money. No sooner would he hang up and light a butt and try to relax than the phone would ring again. It was his girlfriend this time, with whom he also had several kids, calling about the same issues, and the shouting started all over.

I knew Gordy's whole sordid history, including his bank balance, just from sitting at the bar having a nightly bowl of spaghetti and a beer. Gordy would ask me, Need another beer? What am I going to do? Jesus Christ! Usually I looked up from my spaghetti and suggested suicide or maybe amputating his dick.

Don't think I haven't considered it! he'd shout. *Don't believe for one fucking minute I haven't fucking thought about it!*

Then Marty, his waitress, would come up behind me with another basket of bread and say, Don't tell him those things; I need the job.

S̲ara came to visit for a month every summer. I hired babysitters during the day, took her to the Buffalo Zoo on my days off, and we hung out at night. She never seemed homesick for New Jersey, where she and Judie were living with Judie's parents. If I went back to the aquarium at night to work in the lab I took her along. She learned the names of the fishes she liked, but was especially fascinated by the alligators. We were open late on summer evenings, and patrons often wandered over from the nearby bars. One time a drunk came to the admissions window, paid the full price, used the men's room, and left.

Another time a drunk knocked on the window of the lab and motioned me outside. He said to me, You have aquatic mice. It's a real pisser.

Where? I asked. He led Sara and me to a fish exhibit with a dry diorama behind it, and in the diorama was a mouse sitting atop a head of coral and looking around.

Yep, a real pisser, the drunk repeated, and staggered away down the gallery. I showed the mouse to Sara, who of course wanted to take it home, but the apartment had its own mice. Lots of them.

I later bought an African gray parrot during a trip to England and kept it near a window on a homemade stand. One night I was reading quietly in my chair when a large mouse emerged from a hole in the baseboard and crept under the stand. The parrot watched the mouse a minute, picked up a sunflower seed in its beak, and dropped it on the floor. After eating the seed the mouse stood on its hind legs and looked up, and the parrot dropped another. A pattern was established. Every night the mouse appeared underneath the stand and the parrot fed it. Mice sometimes have long runs along marked scent trails, and I wondered how well this one knew the building.

I put an open paper sandwich bag along the wall near the stand and chased the mouse into it. Under the lamp I could see she was old and tattered and missing most of her tail, and recognizing her would be easy. I released her in the furnace room four stories below and returned to my chair. She was back being fed by the parrot twenty minutes later and was still coming around when the parrot and I moved out a year or so later.

My next residence was in the La Salle section of Niagara Falls on the city's south side. I rented a rundown cottage, bought a car, and commuted to work on the Robert Moses Parkway. The cottage was one of three clustered around a large house where the landlady, a divorced woman named Lucy, lived with her teenage daughter. One of my windows overlooked a small affluent of the Niagara River. Too large to be a creek it was more a slow ditch with steep sides thatched woefully by weeds.

Lucy was usually in her nightgown and toting a cigarette and a drink. She was an easy landlady whose only requirement was to pay the rent on time. Sometimes her boyfriend stopped by in his white uniform and white cap. He was a baker at the Nabisco Shredded Wheat plant that seemed to stick out of the riverbank like a gray middle finger. He worked shift and was usually loaded. I got accustomed to certain noises in the night associated with his visits. Once I looked out the window seeing what resembled an albino buffalo entangled in the clothes lines, enraged and flailing at sheets.

My place had a bedroom, living room, kitchen, pantry, bathroom, and a furnace room with an oil-fired furnace just inside the back door. The floor was yellowed linoleum patterned by years of grime. I bought a used mattress and set it on a sheet of plywood over cinder blocks. A couch and two chairs from the town dump followed. Lucy donated a kitchen table and chair from her basement along with assorted pots and pans, silverware, and unmatched dishes. For distraction I had a radio. Bookshelves of boards and cinder blocks were stacked against a living room wall. With windows on three sides, the pantry was the warmest and brightest room in the house, so I moved my desk there and kept the parrot beside me for company.

I had by now written a book describing the scientific basis of aquarium keeping, nearly a thousand typewritten pages and still incomplete. Something was wrong. Where was the forest among all those trees? I took three nights and read every bloated sentence, finding little discernment in the information, a frost-heave of structure, and lots of bad prose. Afterward I got drunk and threw everything away, and upon sobering up I started over. The final output of that second effort, finally published in 1970, was one hundred and fifty manuscript pages of information succinctly organized and simply told. Whether good or bad it was at least efficient. I'd wanted a long-term project, and from this standpoint the effort was successful: about two years to write the second draft from start to finish, a production of roughly seventy-five pages a year, or slightly more than six pages a month.

Around the time I was finishing up my manuscript I met Carol, an attractive former airline stewardess now working at a travel agency in Niagara Falls. She sold me a plane ticket and we started dating. We spent most of our time in the Falls, although she was living in Hamburg, which was south of Buffalo and a long commute. She moved in almost without my noticing, leaving a few more clothes in the closet over time until eventually they were all there. This was another example of how not thinking about things alters your existence. What to me was casual dating had become serious to her. Nothing, as I recall, had ever been discussed specifically, but there were our shoes lined up side by side, no room on the shelf in the bathroom for my toothbrush, and a voice asking me to take out the garbage where before there had been no garbage because I was still eating at Guarino's.

Most of the women I met in the late sixties seemed to be crazy, Carol being an exception. I remember a flashy redhead at a conference in Chicago who was volunteering for some educational organization and looking like the teacher you never had in school, so I requested a personal tour of the city. We went to Old Town that night where we toured a lot of loud bars. Her name was Cary, and she was secretary to a group of psychiatrists where one of the benefits was free psychotherapy if you needed it, which in Cary's opinion everybody did.

In the early morning we ended up at her apartment. We drank some more while she described in detail her many mental anguishes and how she was still several decades away from ever possessing a functionally rational brain. About then I was straddling that border of inebriation where the larger head could still outthink the one in my pants, and it was telling me to get out of there. I started making appropriate moves in that direction, but then lace panties hit the floor. We skipped the rest of the conference and instead ordered in a lot of Chinese food and assorted mind-altering beverages.

I returned home expecting a routine existence. A couple of days went by and then the letters began to arrive, at least one in every mail, sometimes two or three. Each contained an impression of her parted lips in colorful lipstick. The stationery had faint background images of bunnies and baby bears. Sometimes a letter would say only, I Love Us!!!!! or Thinking Of Us!!!!! with lip smudges obliterating any spaces left over.

Cary also telephoned regularly at night saying that her therapist was trying to fuck her but she was holding out because of our love, even though the experience was guaranteed to advance her progress by six months at least. She flew in unannounced to cook me Thanksgiving dinner, despite my plans to celebrate alone with frozen macaroni. When the turkey emerged from the oven it was no more or less naked than its cook. Cary then served it along with stuffing and gravy while wearing only a frilly apron smothered in tiny red hearts.

Ah, Cary, gorgeous Cary, incurably crazy and quite contrary. After the wedding we would need an actual house, she told me during one visit. Here, look at these pictures I've circled in the real estate ads.

What wedding? I asked.

You and me, she replied, after you get into counseling. Children can't be raised in a dingy apartment overlooking an alley, she continued with a sweep of her arm. Ours, I learned, would be home schooled and reared butt-naked through the teenage years; intensive psychotherapy must commence with the first spoken sentence. Two of each, boys and girls, would be nice, spaced evenly apart. And naturally I would need a better paying job. I was hopelessly behind in this progression, not having made it past that first night in Chicago and the image of pink panties on polished pine. We were smoking in bed during this discussion, and when I failed to respond with suitable enthusiasm she doused me in bourbon, struck match, and tried to light me off like a flambé.

There was Debbie, a dancer and wannabe singer who performed at Ed's Grill where Main Street curved around just before the Rainbow Bridge to Canada. She was young and pretty and moved gracefully as a panther. Sadly, her singing voice was astringent and annoying, and I found it impossible to sit at the bar casting the admiring glances she expected.

Debbie often barged in while I was trying to write or simply think. I listened to sordid stories about what her best friend had done in their youth, but of course this girlfriend had never existed and the stories were entirely autobiographical. One was about an evening when the imaginary friend and her boyfriend tried to descend the stairs locked in flagrant delicto only to bump directly into her parents just home from a movie and ascending the same stairs. The embarrassment, her friend had told Debbie, was so devastating she thought she might never recover. Then Debbie emitted sympathetic sobs. I went along with these deceptions out of apathy, and when we broke up she slashed two of my tires.

Summer nights in Niagara Falls during the sixties were down and dirty. It was impossible to make it to the end of Falls Street having a drink in every bar, and that was without crossing to the other side. The air was heavy with factory smoke, and it stank of chemicals and stale beer, of vomit and piss, and the music blaring through the open doors of bars rattled your teeth. Canadians poured across the Rainbow Bridge on Friday and Saturday nights in search of a good time, and generally they found it.

The bar food was good, and if you were single there was no reason to eat in regular restaurants, shop for groceries, or even own a refrigerator and stove. In late spring, during the years before pollution nearly killed everything, bars offered cold deep-fried smelts from the lower Niagara River as free snacks. They were stacked head-down in beer mugs like greasy pencils, eyes blind and breaded, mouths set in bland asphyxiation. Nearby were bowls of hot sauce for dipping. Many a factory worker never made it home for supper.

You could get a tasty beef-on-weck at any dive in town for next to nothing and eat it while sitting at a bar awash in spilled beer and soapsuds in the company of toothless sages. The best came from a joint near Hyde Park where the beef was tender and ladled in pieces onto the kummelweck roll in a natural gravy. Some bars specialized. I knew them all and made the rounds after work, depending on what I craved on a particular evening. There was Italian at Guarino's, of course, and Greek at the Alpine across Third Avenue. The Green Lantern offered a mean burger.

For upscale dining nothing could top Pete's Market on Pine Avenue where the featured dinner was a salad, T-bone steak, and baked potato for two bucks. I took a girl there one night on a first date. We got a table near a window and ordered drinks. Just as they arrived a guy came through the door with a pump-action shotgun thinking to catch his wife with another man. She wasn't there, but he shot up the bar anyway, blasting the mirror and bottles in front of it to tiny pieces. The bartender ducked for cover and so did we, diving under the table and hoping to become small among the chair legs.

The shooter left and the cops came, and my date said, This is much too exciting for me, 'bye, and she stepped outside and hailed a taxi. She was actually from Buffalo, and I never saw her again.

I often had beers after work at the Press Box, joining the journalists who labored on the Niagara Falls *Gazette*, one being John Hanchette, my age and just starting his career too. On spring nights we blocked open the door to let out cigarette smoke and the exhaust from windpipes, looking through it now and then on snow still hunkered in the crotches of curbs. Any breeze carried a nocturnal factory halitosis that crept up from the river like a crude and secretive beast, rubbing its scent against the stained bricks of the buildings, the skeletal trees. If you lived in the Falls you thought the whole world smelled that way.

In a profession where words are often a dull form of silence, John listened to his inner poet and made music. Sometimes the risks were too good not to take. I was working in the lab one evening when he called from the newsroom. He was finishing his account of an interview with Mayor E. Dent Lackey for the next day's edition of the *Gazette*. There had been rumors of sycophants wanting to place a statue of the mayor in one of our city parks, and when John asked him about this the mayor had seemed uncharacteristically humble, saying he was thrilled by the idea but couldn't possible accept such an honor.

It seemed a strange response from a man who liked to lead parades down Main Street dressed completely in white and riding a white horse, snow-white hair buffed to high gloss and flashing a fish-eating grin. Mayor Lackey referred to opponents as those goddamn sons of bitches and once admonished a constituent at an open meeting to stop trying to sell him a bushel of shit. He was outrageous, and the citizens of Niagara Falls loved him. Quite a step up from his former job as an ordained Methodist minister. After his wife Zelda died, and following an interlude of confused redundancy, he married her twin sister.

I'll probably be fired, John told me that evening, but I'm trying like hell to slip this headline past the copy editor: Mayor Fights Erection in Hyde Park.

*T*he Vietnam War was the most important event of my generation, rolling across us like a tidal wave, but UD and I had been down too deep and felt only a vague rocking motion. UD avoided the draft, and I was never called. Cap had surfed the crest. After leaving Beach Haven in the fall of 1962, Cap and UD made their ways separately to California, meeting up in Los Angeles. When Cap's draft notice arrived offering the prospect of a lengthy adrenaline high he tuned in, turned on, and signed up. The war, of course, was a metaphorical body bag zipped shut over the living and dead alike, enclosing all who participated in a psychedelic nightmare. It was everything he wanted, and when that tour ended he went to OCS, emerged a mustang lieutenant, and couldn't wait to get back. As Churchill said, nothing is more exhilarating than to be shot at without result, this being especially true in Vietnam where the generals were stoned on power and everyone else was just stoned.

I was still living in the Falls when Cap mustered out and with nowhere better to go he moved there too. He went to work managing the city's biggest nightclub, called the Speakeasy, a sprawling old place in the north end with a roaring twenties motif. It was great fun, and Cap's electric personality made the place hustle and jump. His girlfriend Harriet, also free of the Army, came along. I was living with Carol, and the four of us often went places together and hung out. We drank outrageous amounts of alcohol, except Carol, who was allergic to it and didn't drink at all.

Those who knew Cap believed the war had left him unscarred. This was hardly the case. Beneath the laughter and good times lay a dark malignancy. In Cap's case the emptiness had always been there, and Vietnam plugged the last exit to salvation. The war experiences stayed and dissolved slowly through his psyche opening new channels of pain, different avenues of anguish. Booze offered temporary elation, a poor simulation of how combat made your ears pound and sphincter tighten, but any rush was better than none, so he upped the dosage. As Mia Couto wrote, War is a snake that bites us with our own teeth.

The Vietnam rush had been terrific, the cost steep, and now faces of dead comrades surfaced relentlessly. He floated a layer of alcohol above their memories, which worked until dawn when nothing remained but the horror itself, photographs lining a corridor of nightmares. Through it all he was expected to function: go to work, pay the bills, behave normally, order eggs scrambled with bacon well done. And smile. No one could do this without screaming or staying drunk, and to scream meant admitting the hurt.

Some of this sadness was about the death of experience. The war could never be reprised, and so he moved as a shape-shifter among us dressed in a mask uncomfortably like our own. Vietnam had been a televised event, America's first war brought live to uninterested citizens sitting down to watch the evening news. For most, the conflict lasted exactly thirty minutes a day starting at six o'clock.

The VA psychiatrists prescribed meds for PTSD, which helped some and kept him drugged, but psychotherapy had proved useless. On the desk lay his life in a file folder, thin-edged and rectangular, a character out of *Flatland*, that fictive place minus a third dimension: heart and guts clipped inside, penciled notes like veins and arteries. Think hard among the walls painted institutional green and you had a Vietnamese shit field; pop enough Valium and the scuffed linoleum became red clay. You looked up at this shrink person, or maybe in a mirror, and asked the obvious question: who the hell *are* you?

Meds deepened the drunks, made them richer and more efficient, until blackouts became common. He awoke in jail or in different cities, or in the jails of different cities, not caring. Harriet left. So did other women, some of whom he actually knew. It was simple, really: reach for the cunt and pull it down over your ears until the sounds of terror and death and boredom drift away.

Everything touched a live wire of memory, even rain. Tropical rain dripping off your helmet trickled down your legs and onto the ground, overflowed into streams then into rivers, and these in turn overflowed until the land everywhere dissolved in liquid brown covered over by gray mist. The skin on your feet turned pasty white like that of a floating corpse. It swelled and sloughed until you could peel it off in layers, bleached and spongy and turgid. You felt as if you could wrap your hands around your feet and squeeze out the water, making them thin and smooth again. If the skin didn't come off outright it rotted away. Maybe going barefoot was the answer because boots and socks kept in the wetness and heat, encouraging things to grow as in a Petri dish. Fungi sent mycelia underneath the toenails turning them black, prying them loose until they fell off to be found later inside your socks. Even scratching your feet was an edgy proposition. Suppose you scratched too hard or grabbed an ankle and pushed down making everything slide off, including the flesh all the way to the toes, and suddenly you were looking at rain-slicked bones. That was one nightmare.

During monsoon season the ground turned to viscous mud that consorted with gravity to suck at boots, gripping them like a stubborn octopus. Then came the dry season when the clay became powder. The paddies shriveled and shrank, their bottoms cracking into spider-web patterns seen on old porcelain; days and nights when the heat sat on your chest like a sweating buffalo and your mouth was too desiccated to spit. The APCs came to resemble dirty red beetles cooked hot in the sun and short-tempered like the men who rode them, growling at everyone and blistering the skin of the unwary.

Death is for everyone, its biology universal. It's the prelude that hurts, not dying in the rain. With faltering of the brain's neurocircuitry the awake mind enters a circumstantial dream of imploding images. Objects fade, reducing wetness to a primal sensation. You're riding it now, a train wreck of upside-down scenes back-projected onto dimming retinas, the personal entertainment system devised by evolution for killing time in death's waiting room. Then the door opens and everything gets sucked through blinding whiteness, the white flash right before endless black: God's putative face or else some hallucinatory climax in monochrome backed by outgoing one fifty-fives. Flares light up the damp sky, but you don't see them. They fall in slow wobbles on their parachutes, squeaking like rusty screen doors or frenetic mice. Maybe, Cap told me, I should have died there too.

Secondhand memories of soldiers whose faces and names I never knew fade in and out of Cap's stories. The men stand quietly as scarecrows, poseurs of the interrupted gesture, one with an arm raised aimlessly, another bent over in mirth, still another slapping the back of a comrade. Shadowless silhouettes waiting for death against a green hillside, in Vietnam or someplace else. Nothing seems real, not the past where constructivist dreams disrupt gravity and motion and we believe we can see the hooves of running horses, the spokes of spinning wheels. Sound disconnects from image; streaking military jets are fragments of context pinned against the clouds. Artillery subsides to sensation, a thudding in the bones, vibrations such as worms feel in the hardening ground. The hills have wounds on their flanks. Never mind that nearby a mouth opens but no scream emerges. Maybe it's yours.

At the end what is it that bends down to kiss its ass good-bye? Could this be the soul? Glance at mortality's scorecard and think: I promise to quit drinking and chasing after nooky, if not forty years ago then now, right now. Whoever you are up there please give me just another year, month, day. . . . That distant noise, artillery or thunder? Or God shaking the ground like he's gathering in a picnic blanket and snapping off the crumbs. Someone else's voice inside your head. It mutters distractedly, Fucking ants.

12

*J*udie had been pregnant when she finally left for good and moved back to New Jersey. She named our son Michael. His birth was still a month away. It was April 1968, and the Universe was flying apart. Martin Luther King had just been assassinated in Memphis. Two days later race riots broke out, and orange flames feasted on the night skies of our cities. It all seemed part of a natural pattern: that January when the Tet Offensive exploded across Vietnam I couldn't stop thinking about Cap somewhere in the belly of the dragon, insane on nicotine and adrenaline. In New York, I learned much later, Uncle D. had become hooked on heroin and taken to raging through the streets with other war protestors, pelting the cops with spring flowers. Bobby Kennedy would be shot dead in June, and in the political maelstrom that followed came Hanchette's reports to the *Gazette* from Chicago's Democratic National Convention, written in air thick with tear gas and the whiff of nightsticks. For my part I decided to drop over the edge of the world, and the closest edge I knew was Mexico.

I needed a break to shove personal and world events to the side; I needed space to think. But I also went to Mexico to forget about the science of the sea and put before me once again memories of its languid moods and cold wet rhythms. In the frenzy of everyday living these had ceased to occupy my thoughts until I forgot the feel of surf, the taste of salt, and awoke each morning having dreamed only information from books. Information and images of fishes behind glass walls.

To rekindle those earlier feelings I sought a desiccated unfamiliar land of hidden water that in my earliest recollections had flowed through subterranean channels accessible only to the imagination. There among burning hills the dry would make poignant the wet, or so I hoped. It was an ancient place once called Tlalocan, a mythical Eden ruled by the goddess Chalchiuhtlicue where mountains barely visible are vases of water. One day the shriveled stones that hold their form will shatter and all of us will be swept away.

Having arrived in Guadalajara on an evening flight I bought some tortillas from a street vendor and looked for a place to sleep. A park bench seemed suitable, although its form was curved to fit the sigmoid shape of a sitting person, which left the flat portion barely wide enough for me to lie on my side. Still, I fell asleep in minutes, lulled by the distant barking of dogs and the soft conversations of late-night strollers. Their forms seemed ghostly as I drifted off, voices without the sound of footfalls.

The next morning I took a taxi to Mercado Liberidad, Guadalajara's gigantic open-air market. From a visit the previous year I remembered a bilingual green parrot owned by one of the vendors. It had stood among a pile of serapes and sombreros and screamed alternately at passersby, *¡Hijo de puto!* and Son of a whore! But this time the vendor was not there. No one recalled his name or where he had gone, but everyone knew about the parrot.

Yes, *señor*, that was a fine parrot, said a toothless old woman who now occupied the space. She sold tiny wooden replicas of the Virgin, displaying them on a card table in perfect rows like toy soldiers. She fussed over them nervously, whispering a short prayer with every adjustment. Then she looked at me through filmy corneas. But it was loud and dirty, that parrot. Some people around here didn't like it and were glad to see it go. Me? I learned long ago not to complain. She uttered a proverb about flies not entering a closed mouth, then crossed herself.

I needed supplies, and the stalls were endless. Eventually everything was assembled: a serape for the cold nights, an off-white cotton shirt and matching pants worn by the campesinos, a straw sombrero to keep away the sun. I bought a long length of rope, a sack of dried beans and another of rice, a large can of coffee, a knife and fork, a tin cup and plate to match, a small aluminum pot with a lid, some tins of boiled ham, and several dented canteens of dull aluminum. In my knapsack was a long-sleeved shirt, two pairs of shorts, socks, underwear, a razor, tee-shirts, two large handkerchiefs to serve as bandanas, pocket knife, hatchet, a stick of deodorant, a bar of soap in a plastic container, zinc oxide, sunglasses, aspirin, a toothbrush and toothpaste, antibiotics, and flea powder. I was wearing the rest: hiking boots, jeans, and a tee-shirt.

I found a vacant corner and changed into my new campesino clothes then took a taxi to the city limits and started walking south. Rain had not fallen in months. The air tasted gritty and soon covered me in a patina of dust. Exhaust fumes skulked close to the ground, the only breeze an intermittent blast off the macadam from a passing vehicle. Road heat radiated into my feet until they were wet through and mushy and began to skate around inside the boots. By noon the sky had domed up, a radiant blue parabola marred only by black flecks of vultures, and where its edges bent low the horizon fractured into plates of shimmering heat. I had in my backpack a little book of Mexican proverbs, one of which read, For those who want the blue sky, the price is expensive.

In mid-afternoon an ancient stake bed pulled to the side and stopped. Its cargo of campesinos shifted to make a space as I swung aboard. I passed around a pack of American cigarettes. The man nearest me cupped his hands around a match, and when I steadied them with my own they had the feel of dried horn. No one spoke. We stopped at villages where men got off, and by dusk only I was left. The driver leaned out the window and told me that he lived across the road. He offered a meal and a place to sleep.

The next morning I thumbed a ride with another group of field workers in a dilapidated truck. The track followed an alluvial plain eastward along the southern edge of Laguna de Chapala, past hills of metamorphic rock visible farther to the south. Now in the dry season the lake had retracted to a distant orb. Fierce red crabs stalked the mudflats pursuing their medieval jousts, oblivious to creeping fishermen and the lurch of civilization. The truck stopped to turn around at Tuxcueca and I got out. Trees drooped torpidly in what passed for a square, and parked under one of them was an ancient Ford sedan with *Taxi* painted on its sides. On the front seat behind the wheel sat the driver, snoring loudly. I tapped on the roof.

Can I help you, *señor*? He stretched mightily and yawned like a hyena, opening his jaws wider than I thought possible.

I want to hire your taxi.

Yes, I see, you come from *el otro lado*. I must have looked confused. From the United States, he said. Around here we call it the other side. Where do you want to go?

I don't know, I replied. This caught his attention.

You don't know? His brow wrinkled, and he pursed his lips as if deep in thought. Then he turned and looked at me. *Señor*, everybody wants to go somewhere. People hire me to take them to a place, not to take them nowhere.

I didn't say nowhere, I answered, but you must help me decide.

Actually, I had a plan in mind. It was to wander into the dry forests where the trees are short and shrubby and drop their leaves until the rainy season. These deciduous tropical landscapes are extensive, covering about eight percent of Mexico and prevalent along the slopes of the western cordilleras, in particular the Sierra Madre Occidental and the foothills of Jalisco and Michoacán.

Okay, he grunted. With effort he attacked the door, source of his imprisonment, first yanking up the handle while banging it sharply with his left shoulder. On about the third try it yielded with a groan. He leaned toward the passenger side to get a rolling start and propelled himself through the opening and onto his feet. This fucking door, it needs fixing but I have no time.

We unfolded the map on the hood, and I pointed to a likely destination in Michoacán. He studied the end of my finger. *Señor*, that place is empty! I noticed a sliver of harelip hunkered down under three days of whiskers. He was short and overfat and smelled like a goat long in rut, and he wore on his person a large consignment of unholiness. One eye looked directly ahead, but from the other I knew how badly he yearned to talk about women.

Aren't there villages?

Yes, of course, but most are not on your map, just a few huts of the campesinos, maybe a well with a bucket and if you're lucky a small cantina. And maybe the cantina will even have food to sell. And a woman. The wandering eye turned my way slyly.

That's okay, and I also need a horse. I want to rent a horse and ride through the forest.

Excuse me, what's your name, *señor*?

I told him. And yours?

Guillermo. We shook hands.

No disrespect, but you're a crazy gringo, Esteban. The roads there are very bad and sometimes they stop or go nowhere, but I can drive you to the town of Tancítaro just south of Pico Tacítaro where I know some women. Not for me, of course, I am recently a widower, God rest her soul. Because of grief I have been unable to work on my car or even to eat. I'm going mad and losing weight. When I look into the mirror I see a starving dog. He patted his stomach, stunned briefly by mournfulness.

After crossing himself, he continued. From Tancítaro two rivers flow south out of the mountains, and occasionally there are villages. He pointed to them: Pareo, Chondémbaro, Acúmbaro, La Estancia, Parácuaro. But if you get lost you will die of thirst. The land is hot and dry.

I could die of thirst? I was once again getting accustomed to the language and wanted to be certain of his words.

Yes, *señor. Usted podría morirse de sed.*

I have a compass. Can you get me a horse?

My cousin lives near Parácuaro, about two hundred kilometers from here, and he used to have a horse. Now in the dry season he probably isn't working it. We can go there instead of to Tancítaro, but you must pay me to drive you and also pay for the gas and oil both ways. And we need to rent a room somewhere along the way to spend the night, unless we sleep in the car. This is not a fast trip with the awful roads and my poor car needing many repairs. If only I had the time. He exhaled the sadness of a beached porpoise.

We agreed on a price, and I tossed my knapsack onto the backseat. No sooner had I got in beside Guillermo than he turned chummy. We were now comrades of the open road, and he immediately addressed me using the familiar *tú* instead of the formal *usted*. He pumped the accelerator several times to prime the carburetor then stepped on the starter button, driving birds in the branches overhead to tremors of cacophonous pity. The bucks and spasms followed by plumes of wrenching black smoke were signs of an engine sliding expectantly toward burial in some metallic bone yard. The muffler could evidently relate its own tragic history, having been shed in a distant mechanical ecdysis and leaving behind an open wound no doubt gangrenous with rust. Guillermo pointed out the utility of the holes in the floor by spitting through one between his feet.

We must find some women soon to cool my hot blood, he said to me, evidently his great foreign hope.

I thought you were mourning your dead wife.

Ah, you misunderstood, Señor Esteban, probably because

you speak Spanish so poorly. It's the same with all gringos. He shook his head at this profound mystery. If my wife were truly dead I could never leave the cemetery for grieving. I would die there, food for the vultures. Such a saintly woman, my Teresa! But fortunately she's alive and healthy, no doubt praying to the Virgin as we speak and lighting a candle for our safe trip. He pursed his lips to stimulate a fresh upwelling of memories. But she's back in Tuxcueca and I'm here. What we need now, because we're men, is *la panocha*. How do you say this in English?

Pussy.

Poosy. *Poosy*! He pounded the steering wheel. *Poosy*! Soon I'll be speaking perfect English while you, my friend, will still speak Spanish like a *pendejo*. His cackling was like harried fowl penned inside a steel barn. Do you have a cigarette? Travelers should share everything—cigarettes, tequila, even women.

Did you bring along anything to share?

Of course! He opened the glove box and lifted out a bottle. Don't be disappointed, my friend. Tequila doesn't have the worm at the bottom. That's mescal, but only gringos like drinking worms. There's a little left, perhaps a swallow for each of us. He took a big one and handed me the remainder.

His wandering eye left the road and gathered me in. I've been drinking more than usual since the death of my dear wife Juanita. Ah, you finished it! No problem, Esteban, except that was the last of my tequila. It was the best, very expensive. Now that you have drunk my last drop you can buy the next bottle. Do you have a match? This cigarette you've given me is unlikely to light itself.

We followed the lake east before veering away south toward Sahuayo de Morelos, the largest town I'd seen since Guadalajara. The plain was merging with foothills, and the car was laboring to climb even the lowest of them, often wheezing nearly to a stop. We pulled into a filling station in town to refuel. Every tank of gas was also taking a quart of oil. This time I bought a half-dozen cans of STP and poured one of them in with the oil in an attempt to gum up the pistons and perhaps gain some cylinder compression. I also bought a bottle of tequila, Mexican cigarettes, some cigars, two Cokes, and a few packages of crackers. From an outdoor vendor across the street we picked up some hot tortillas wrapped around an indifferent stuffing of greasy meat and peppers. After a piss against the back wall of the filling station we set off again.

Guillermo, a cabalist and professed authority even in everyday matters, was in the habit of placing a forefinger just underneath his eye before speaking, a studied mannerism probably borrowed from someone formerly admired, maybe a priest or politician. He was doing this when he remarked, Señor Esteban, why are you always reading that little book?

It's a dictionary. I'm learning words in Spanish.

Ah! You need to know a word? Just ask me. Ask me, Guillermo, How do you say . . . and then point to what you want to know.

But suppose the word isn't an object but a thought? If I can't tell you the thought, how can I ask what word describes it?

He pursed his lips. Yes, this is true. So, how long before you learn to speak Spanish?

I'm speaking it right now.

You call what you say speaking Spanish? You talk worse than a campesino. Only someone like me, a cultured man, could ever understand you, and I can do it only because of immense experience and my friendship with many important gringos. He lifted his right butt cheek and farted delicately.

At least I try. Can you speak English?

Guillermo twisted back and forth on the seat, clearly annoyed. You think I can't learn English? Who is ever here to help? You, for example? I've asked you many times to teach me.

You've never asked me, and we just met this morning. Have a cigar.

He put the cigar in his mouth and leaned in my direction for a light. Perhaps not, but I'm asking you now.

You could buy a dictionary and learn the English words.

He waved a hand as if brushing away a fly. No, Señor Professor. Unlike you I'm a man of action and adventure. Men such as I learn best from experience, no books are necessary.

I could teach you songs to sing to your children.

His mobile eye wandered over to my side and squinted. Okay, I have something to say to you, my friend. How do you say in English, *chingate*?

Fuck you.

Exactly! *Fuck you*. That's how I feel right now, at this very minute. What can I say to go with it?

You want to make it stronger, an even better fuck you? I stuck up my middle finger.

He clenched the cigar in his teeth. Okay, Señor Esteban, *poosy* and *fuck you*, and he removed both hands from the steering wheel and flashed me a double bird. You see? Ha! In only a minute I speak English better than you speak Spanish. Never forget that I'm very intelligent. *Tu andas con mal tapon.*

I was confused by this last sentence. It could mean I was constipated, which no gringo ever is in Mexico, or its literal meaning, that I was walking around with a defective cork. I asked Guillermo to explain. He sighed at my stupidity. It's an expression we use around here. It means you have a tight ass. What's the problem? he asked crossly. Isn't this in your dictionary?

Fuck you, I said, and he laughed.

We came to a village that evening. Guillermo approached one of the huts and said something, and shortly a woman came out of the dusk with a plate of tortillas and cold beans. I paid her, and we ate silently on the hood of the car. Afterward we drew a bucket of water from the well and washed the dust from our heads and arms, had a large swallow of tequila each, took a piss on the tires, and went to sleep in the car.

As I was drifting off Guillermo asked if I had a wife. I told him I didn't know. He sat up and peered at me with his straight-ahead eye. You don't know if you have a wife? First you don't know where you want to go, now this. You are very confused, *señor*. Was it another man? he asked.

Maybe, I replied. Who ever knows? Women. You can't live with them and you can't, how do you say, BANG! I pointed the pistol of my forefinger at his nose.

He laughed and lay back on the front seat. Women require what men like us can't provide, Señor Esteban, and that's the endless confession of love. It's best to love a woman only until your own love wears out, like a tire.

Judie and I had quarreled viciously for months until in a fit of howling poignancy I stuffed her into the basket we used as a clothes hamper. Lust reverted to boredom, disagreements to active dislike, and we finally parted as gulls do after squabbling over some rotten inedible thing. Here on Guillermo's sprung back seat I retained the memory of noise but not of conversation, and even that seemed muted.

Judie had acquired possessions with that great avarice of the debtor and lived comfortably among clutter and unwashed dishes. In contrast, each object I owned had become a Lilliputian mooring line, subtracting its weight in freedom and prognosticating death by immobility, suffocation in the midst of silent screams. One night I came home drunk and tripped over a chair newly moved to a different location. I got up and smashed it flat. You were loaded, Judie said to me the next day, why take it out on a chair? She didn't understand that the enemy had now been reduced by one.

After this episode I could sense the furniture stalking me, flaunting its brave Naugahyde or skulking behind reedy hordes of faux beach grass. Fabric lions replicated beyond any hope of extinction; tiny green vines rippled along the curtains in Brownian movements of dread. My true desire was to own nothing and sleep on a park bench. When we separated I gave Judie everything without argument, even the car. I received her debts in return, although I really wanted my daughter, then three, but the court believed firmly that children should remain with their mothers. Several years later, upon splitting from Carol, my second wife, I again relinquished everything in gratitude. She left behind a dog named Munchkin and an empty house, neither of which she considered portable. Munchkin and I happily slept on the floor and scavenged from cans.

We passed through Apatzingán the next afternoon. As before we bought tortillas from a street vendor while replenishing the car's fluids, and again spent the night sleeping on the seats, this time along a side road that led to Chiquihuitillo. The next morning we finally came to Parácuaro and continued north until reaching a dusty farm straddling what remained of the road. I got out after arranging with Guillermo to pick me up in nine days, give or take a day, and walked up to the hut just as its owner appeared in the doorway. Guillermo was not to leave until I waved.

The campesino listened to me and said, I don't know anyone named Guillermo, *señor*.

He's your cousin, and he says that you have a horse.

I have no cousin named Guillermo, but I have a horse. That's him. He pointed at a horse standing in a paddock across the road. We went over to see. The horse was bony and fly-troubled with hide like a patchy old rug scuffed by years of dirty boots. His head hung listlessly, the only movement an intermittent twitch of an ear.

Does this horse have a name?

A name, *señor*?

What do you call him?

We don't call him anything. He's just a horse.

I'll call him Rocinante.

My companion seemed puzzled. That's a good name, *señor*, if you think he needs a name. Unlike Guillermo he spoke in the manner of most Mexicans, polite and self-effacing. I knew nothing about horses, but as a kid I'd watched lots of cowboy movies. Horses in the movies never ate, at least within view of the audience. Evidently the sight of horses eating was thought to be unpleasant or boring.

I want to rent your horse. Can you also sell me some grain to feed him?

I can spare a little, *señor*. I'll put it in this grain sack, but please return the sack to me. I don't have another one.

The dog that had been sleeping in the paddock was now awake and sniffing my boots. Like the horse it was nondescript and bony.

Is this your dog?

No, *señor*. It's nobody's dog.

The previous spring Cap, Harriet, her mama, and I had rented horses for the day in Jocotepec, a village on Laguna de Chapala, at a peso each. I offered Rocinante's owner five pesos a day with another three pesos for the grain, giving him the price for seven days in advance, the balance to be paid at the end of the trip. He seemed pleased and thanked me several times.

I barely listened as the conversation changed, watching instead his calloused feet in the dust, seeing the top of his shabby straw sombrero on the bent-over head. The space between action and words had disconnected. He suddenly stood straight and walked into his hut, emerging a moment later with a greasy paper bag.

Here, *señor*, please take this with you.

What is it?

It's for the horse. He's very nervous away from home. I must have looked puzzled because he cupped his hands around his mouth and made gentle blowing sounds.

I unrolled the bag and looked inside. It was stuffed with dried marijuana, mostly flowers, not sorted and cleaned but chopped crudely into large pieces. There was also a pack of smudged rolling papers. I put the bag in my knapsack still unsure of its intended purpose.

We folded an old blanket in half, threw it on Rocinante's back, and secured it with a rope tied underneath his belly. I rigged other ropes for the knapsack, feed sack, and my long rope coiled tightly. Rocinante was wearing a halter to which his owner attached a bridle without a bit. There was nothing more to do or say. I waved to Guillermo, clambered uncertainly onto my steed, and we set off at a stumbling walk in search of a windmill. The dog stopped scratching himself and followed. I decided to call him Sancho Panza.

If possible I would avoid the towns, stopping in the villages only for food and water. The plan was never intended as an underfinanced expedition of self-discovery or a whining crawl into the primitive womb of nature in vogue among the hippies, but simply to wander across a dry landscape far from the sea. I would start by going north, away from Parácuaro where the good road had ended a ways back. The road ahead remained barely recognizable for several more kilometers, terminating at La Estancia. Past this point were trails. The distance and destination were unimportant; it was the moment that mattered, this vista followed by the next, all of it unreliable.

At mid-afternoon I passed a well and stopped to water the animals. The horse was hot but not lathered because all we had done was walk, and it was all I intended to do. Having the riding skills of a tin soldier, anything more and I would have fallen off. Just before sunset I veered into the sparse forest where dead leaves and twigs crunched under us, not stopping until the road was out of sight. Green, the prevalent color of vegetable life, had slunk away from this place taking along its sappy turgidity. Leafless now, the forest lacked visual depth, and what remained had a peculiar flatness of stiff and repetitious shadows mired in skinny impoverishment. A northeastern hardwood forest has a certain fullness even in winter, a confident prosperity, not the starved disheveled look of this one.

Everything being new and strange, I needed daylight to perform the tasks I would later be able to complete in twilight. I took off Rocinante's blanket, which was foul and sweaty, and flung it over a bush hoping it would dry quickly in the low humidity. Next I fixed one end of the long rope bought at the market to Rocinante's halter and the other end to a stout tree using a loop tied with a bowline that would slide in whatever lateral direction he walked. I was finding that boats and horses have certain maintenance factors in common, except that boats are more comfortable and able to go without food. I fed Rocinante some grain from my cupped hands letting what spilled fall back into the bag on the ground. The rope's radius came up short of the campsite so I wouldn't be stepped on in my sleep. I'd accidentally chosen a place that had once been seeded with thatching grass for livestock, tufts of which were still thick enough to keep the horse occupied for several hours.

Some distance away I made a triangle of stones and built a fire in the center. There was plenty of firewood: deadfalls and the broken branches of trees and shrubs were everywhere. I cooked some rice and beans together in the pot and spooned them up, leaving a portion for Sancho Panza. A little coffee and a cigarette and all was well.

The moon rose, a clean ignorant moon far from books and everything I knew. Bleached limbs of trees became bones in the colorless light, the dry forest a botanical ossuary. Branches and trunks stood impassively or leaned or lay flat, often in tangled groups but also in pairs and alone. Neither their positions nor the choice of companionship was ever an option. They lay where they had fallen like the dead on a battlefield, victims of wind and sun and the jaws of termites.

Control over death is illusory. Would I die young in Mexico or old in a distant bed? I'd already decided how little such things matter, that no gods oversee this celestial plantation, that the objective should be to live *and* die. There isn't a lot of introspection among the young, and what they sometimes believe to be a thoughtful pause is often just constipation or the uncertainty that precedes low panic. It takes years to realize nobody gives a shit what you think. I didn't know this at the time. Nothing out there but the galloping blackness, I said to Sancho Panza, who continued to lick his balls stoically and without remorse.

A Mexican proverb states that each of us has his own way of killing fleas. My preference was by chemistry. I lowered my campesino's trousers and dusted my genitals with flea powder, hiked up the pants and dusted my legs, held up the shirt and dusted my chest. Then I dusted the dog. The horse blanket felt drier. I spread it out between the rocks, dragged over the knapsack for a pillow, and pulled the serape over myself. Sancho Panza snuggled closer in the cooling air, an act of little comfort to our poisoned fleas seeking less contaminated worlds. I took a final glance at the sack of grain tied securely in a tree and went to sleep.

Rocinante's nickering awoke me. He was pulling at the end of the rope stretched taut and slipping sideways in clumsy steps. The moon was high and leaning to wane. I lay still while his agitation grew, finally understanding. There was nothing left except to get up, roll a joint, and light it. Then I pulled Rocinante's head down next to mine, cupping a hand around my mouth and blowing smoke up his nostrils in alternate tokes, one for each of us. The minutes grew longer and passed by as if riding the wheels of a faraway train.

I rolled a second joint and lit that one too. Moonlight gathered in Rocinante's eyes, and his demons departed with long sighs. Once inside a cave in Baja I heard a similar sound as if the Minotaur had just awoken from a delicious dream, but it was merely the sea expelling its breath through tone holes in the rocks. Rocinante laid his chin on my shoulder. We stood like that a long time, silent and pensive in new fellowship, settled over by a fetching sorrow.

13

The trail pieced into the end of the road contained a palpable wriggle, loopy and twisted as a shit-out tapeworm. There was forever a rise in front and the one behind just passed over, spaced like the reaches of ocean swells. Dust pooled everywhere waiting to be fluidized by the coming rains. The absence of a saddle and stirrups had brought an unpleasant surprise, that of being unable to rise up and separate my backside from Rocinante's spinous processes that poked up through his uncushioned hide and the thin blanket, jabbing into private and hurtful places. If I leaned forward my flattened scrotum felt every lurch of his unstable gait; leaning back caused a painful stridulation as human coccyx grated across a washboard of lurching horse bone. Squeezing my knees together jockeylike in an effort to lift my ass higher offered no relief, resulting only in aching thighs rubbed red on the insides.

The way threaded through desiccated foothills of dwarfed and wizened vegetation, past humorless lizards the color of stone. The flora seemed dominated by papilionoid legumes such as acacias and mesquites, leafless now with spent pods that rattled dryly in the wind. New leaves would appear after the first rains followed by explosions of peculiar butterfly-shaped flowers. The only shade was beneath low outcroppings.

In late afternoon I came to several huts clustered around a large tamarind where the inhabitants gathered shyly in doorways to gawk. I stopped at the tree and dismounted. A woman emerged from one of the huts, grabbed Rocinante's bridle, and led him away to be watered. Sancho Panza followed them. I lay down under the tree, the only shade I had seen all day. Presently the woman returned. It would soon be dark, and I decided to stay the night. I sat up and asked her if there was food.

I have some tortillas, and I can kill a chicken for you.

I agreed and stretched out again. Ants roamed single file across my chest, evidently accepting me as part of the landscape. Sancho Panza settled in to have a scratch, and we dozed. At sunset the woman brought out a plate containing the chicken and two tortillas, but there was no coffee. I offered to make some for us both, which she declined politely saying it was not necessary. I ate everything on the plate except the carcass and skin, and these I gave to Sancho Panza.

Rocinante had been tied to a post behind the hut. There was no pasturage nearby, so I fed him some grain from my hands and left him content in the company of a donkey. I took the knapsack, serape, horse blanket, and dog and walked over a rise to make camp where the huts were no longer visible, a decision based mostly on dysentery. I thought about the slurry of eyeless organisms living smugly inside my frenzied colon and vowed to shit them out on flat rocks to bake in the sun. Squats had been frequent, dropping trousers to ankles and stepping forward crablike with every squirt. Call it scuttling revenge.

The next morning after watering Rocinante and feeding him some grain I bought several tortillas from the woman and had two of them with coffee at the campsite. We departed in the still-cool air, striding into a landscape the monotony of which seemed to rule out mutability. The stones might have looked eternal, but simply stepping on one altered its features, and turning it over exposed it to a new state of ordinariness. Every raindrop and breath of wind, each particle of airborne dust that abraded against the stones and hillsides degraded them imperceptibly, shrinking them, changing them forever.

Soon the sun exploded over the brown hills, making land and sky simmer. Flies settled on our faces where they feasted on oils and salts and sucked what moisture they could find; gnats ringed our eyes like wildebeests around a putrid waterhole. Today I recall these events clearly, although nothing of the discomfort. Sensations, which stand apart from memory, can't be stored because the moment of experience consumes them as quickly as leaves thrown on a fire. Memories, the remnants of associated circumstances, tend to discount physical pain and indeed all related sensations. We can reconstitute the emotional hurt of a lost love but not the physiological hurt of a lost finger.

In the knapsack was a notebook with the pages still blank. I should be keeping a journal, I told myself, but my fear was the opposite of Sartre's. In recording everyday events the commonplace becomes strange in its very banality: the pockmarks on skin seen at close range, a blue sky that turns sinister after relentless description.

And what is it we see? We look down on our lives, which like the mottled backs of fishes camouflage truth against the darkness below, each of us his own unreliable narrator. Our stories are destitute, tainted by metaphor and held in secret until reassembled later from slippery fragments. We store almost nothing in permanent memory, leave no records of our fears, fantasies, doubts, moments of exhilaration. What we say to others is filtered, altered, and ultimately misinterpreted, although any of us would be hard pressed to repeat any phrase exactly, to string together the same sentence in the same way using identical inflections. Inherited is the capacity to remember but not memory itself, those random pictures and dreams swept up in the ebb and flow of neurotransmitters. We see without comprehension, speak without transcending ignorance, hear what we think we understand.

On that night and all subsequent nights Rocinante and I got stoned, or as the Mexicans say, *Nosotros nos acostamos con rosemaria*, or, we went to bed with rosemary (the herb). We looked at the stars while I wondered if Atlas had allowed his fingers to penetrate the world like a bowling ball. I asked Rocinante, was one thumb stuck deep in the Mariana Trench, the other in Amazonian ooze? Could he have heard the continental plates grind against his ear, feel the Arctic ice on his neck, smell the montane flowers? On exactly what was he standing? And through all this, where was the wind? Rocinante had no answers, and neither did I.

On the fifth day we reached the easternmost river Guillermo had mentioned. It was warm and sluggish, shallow now in the dry months, and I stayed in it most of the afternoon. I washed the dust from Rocinante and Sancho Panza, then from my clothes and from me. I rinsed the horse blanket too, and threw it and the clothes over some bushes in the sun. I decided to spend the night and collected enough wood to keep a fire going for several hours. The hatchet had seldom been needed because many branches from the forest floor were small and brittle enough to snap apart, and once ignited the mesquite burned hot with a low flame. Although grasses were uncommon in the dry forest, enough grew along the bank to provide decent grazing for one horse, so I released Rocinante some distance downstream at the end of his long rope. In the evening I would move him closer to the campsite, giving him still more grazing opportunities.

With exception of a few insects the river held little evidence of aquatic life. Surely there were fishes and probably crayfishes too, but they stayed out of sight. I filled the pot with river water and after letting it settle a couple of hours carefully decanted it into the canteens, nearly all of which were empty. I threw away the sediment, poured all the decanted water back into the pot, boiled it for fifteen minutes, and refilled the canteens, throwing them into the river afterward to cool. It was good to be near water. I felt balanced and normal as if the high stored quality of reason had come into view as payment for the ache, itch, or burn at every personal crevice and rounded surface.

A full day or so had been spent fixating on the notion of transience and the ephemeral evidence organic life leaves behind. Here we were, three complex creatures traversing the land like hunter-gatherers followed only by footprints soon covered over, some molecules of exhaled carbon dioxide, drops of evaporated sweat and urine, and the occasional turd. Even our body odors dissipated quickly as if we had never existed. A record of passing requires tangible evidence in the form of a fossil, a pyramid, a book, an IRS return: something you could see or touch. We were leaving almost nothing behind, and for some reason this bothered me.

Only ignorance gives the illusion of time marching in place. I could sense the world winding down, slowing to the gait of a horse picking its way slowly among strewn rocks and thorny branches shaped by the wind. My dry new mind seemed fresh, open, uncluttered, unlike my oceanic mind littered with species names, equations, biological and chemical processes, and presumed insights based on what I knew or wished to understand. I wanted to abandon the biases of intellectual rigor and other flotsam of learning, to experience the world for its colors, contours, spaces, textures. Here isolated acts could be appreciated without the distraction of prior information.

One time I dismounted quietly to watch a lizard stalk an insect, rush it, grasp it, chew briefly, and swallow. This sequence and others of which I was ignorant had a certain Edenic purity that trivializes scientific description. I wanted to subtract myself as observer and dissolve the frantic insecurity that accompanies knowing something but never enough, replaying sensory contact in memory until each image, sound, or odor faded into another, equally fragile, as easily lost, hoping that underneath opaque knowledge lay a glistening new world. And under that perhaps a deeper, not so restless kind of emptiness.

Sancho Panza and I sat in the river contemplating these problems, I wearing only my sombrero and Sancho Panza just his mangy hide. It took until sunset and a couple of joints when hunger overcame us, the satisfaction gained or lost being about equal. As things turned out it was an empty exercise anyway.

The next morning we continued west to the second river, much like the first, and in days following reversed direction and turned east, crossing familiar trails, although at different places. The first of these after the eastern river led south to Acúmbaro, the one after terminated at Acahuato, and due east of Acahuato was Parácuaro and the road leading north to La Estancia.

Late one afternoon I came to a village that had a cantina with a hitching post out front. I tied Rocinante to it and went inside. Some canned goods were displayed on a wall shelf. The floor was packed earth, and there were four tables, half with chairs. A curtain parted in back and a girl of about twelve came out and asked if I needed anything.

Do you have cold beer?

No, *señor*, there's no electricity in this village, but my mother keeps the beer in a hole dug in the ground where it's cool.

Okay, I'll have a bottle of beer.

Please sit at a table. I'll bring it to you and then water your horse.

Please give my dog water too.

Yes, *señor*. And my mother will make you tortillas and beans. Several chickens, hen-pecked and of shabby plumage, gathered around and eyed me in the spirit of expectant mutualism. Sancho Panza returned and sat among them. When the food arrived I rolled a tortilla around some beans and fed it to him. I drank another beer to permanently dislodge the dust, and after wiping my mouth on the last tortilla I tossed it to the chickens.

The color of the land, a sullen dun, is what I remember most, this and my two companions and a sky as deep and empty as the iris of a blue-eyed god. And the sunlight, of course, that in evening lay draped across the purple hills like a wasted pyre. The wind was there or not, but when it blew it carried a weight like something on thick legs coming at you. Here, Guillermo had insisted, lurked death by dryness or snakebite, although I didn't believe it, not any of it. Occasionally the bones of goats, driftwood-white, poked through the brush, but they were thin and brittle, barely organic, as remote from life as the stones. I learned this by watching Sancho Panza, who ignored them completely.

I arrived back at the campesino's farm at mid-afternoon. The man was lounging in his doorway and came out. Guillermo was parked nearby, dozing in his taxi.

The farmer asked, Did you find it, *señor*, what you were looking for?

Yes, I answered. And the dog followed me all the way.

The dog follows the horse, *señor*. They are friends. Where the horse goes, he goes too. He shrugged. Sancho Panza was already back in his customary corner of the paddock, sniffing it thoroughly to be certain no other dog had slept there in his absence. Rocinante appeared anxious to join him. I paid the balance, then untied my things and threw them in the taxi.

*G*uillermo eased his nose over the window edge and blew it at the ground. He told me he's not your cousin, I said scornfully, as if apprising him of a dirty little secret now uncovered.

He ignored my tone, gaining space for rebuttal while layering his comb-over using thumb and forefinger. Of course not, you misunderstood, he replied. I said my cousin knew this man owned a horse, and that's why I brought you here. Another pause, briefer, as his straight-ahead eye in dramatic surprise looked once to each side for eavesdroppers. Finding none, he attacked my presumption with a slow frontal viciousness.

You thought *he* was my cousin? Please, Señor Esteban! My family is not rich, but we are very cultured and respected. This campesino *wishes* he was my cousin because then he would acquire some of our status. He's a . . . how do you say in English, *pinche chúntaro*?

Fucking hillbilly.

Yes, exactly. He stuck a finger in his ear and dug purposefully toward forgotten pain or some valuable event. You see, I came back for you, as I said. We should celebrate with a drink. Sadly, in my haste to reach you I didn't have time to stop for a bottle. We also need gas, oil, and cigarettes. And *poosy*. I love that word. *Poosy*! Anyway, the campesino tells me we can stay the night with him. I've told him already that you'll pay. He was worried about his horse, but I said to him, this Esteban is a very important man *el otro lado*, and if he was planning to steal a horse it would be a good horse, maybe the most expensive in Mexico, not your ugly animal missing his *albondigas*.

His avocados? I asked stupidly.

Guillermo, who had come out of the car, grabbed his balls with both hands and jumped up and down. Then he asked, Did you look for *albondigas* on this horse? Good luck, my friend, because he doesn't have any. Where are your cigarettes?

I paid the farmer for letting us stay the night. I returned his feed sack and gave him the aluminum pot, most of the canteens, and the remainder of my food. He told me his wife would use the beans and rice when making our supper. I also returned his bag of grass, with the exception of several joints required for the drive back to Guadalajara. That night we ate in the hut with its dirt floor swept clean. Children were somewhere around, shocked to stillness like young rabbits. Guillermo was offered their sleeping space and accepted; I slept in the car.

We left in the morning after tortillas and coffee, but not until our host and I had pushed the car an extended distance over the rough terrain while Guillermo sat in the driver's seat popping the clutch. During the last of these sweaty episodes the engine gave several tubercular coughs before hacking out a loathsome cloud of black sputum and finally igniting. Guillermo then held the gas pedal to the floor while the fan belts screamed and went at one another like humping cougars.

We limped in the direction of Guadalajara dragging the noise of a minor train wreck while Guillermo lectured on nuances of the Spanish language. By the next afternoon we possessed a liter of Oaxacan mescal, an amount guaranteed to surrender all erudition and make even social farting respectable. He poked at my deficient language skills as a skunk harasses a trash can, one being the inability to roll r's. Ah, Esteban my friend, your tongue is stuck to the roof of your mouth (*su lengua se pega al tejado de su boca*). Maybe someday you'll speak like a cultured person and not a gringo who comes to Mexico, gets diarrhea (*obraderas*) like any tourist, and then must stop every kilometer along the road so as not to shit his pants. Stop, Guillermo! he shouted in falsetto. Please stop before it's too late! Ah, but at least we saw the countryside from a horse.

We? I replied. I reached behind and got out my little book of Mexican proverbs. Here's a proverb for you and your manly asshole: *Como dijo la mosca, Andamos arando.*

Guillermo's traveling eye turned vicious, and he snatched away the mescal. So how do you say that in English?

Says the fly (evidently riding on an ox), *We* are plowing this field. I retrieved the mescal and took a righteous swallow.

At that moment Guillermo's attention was diverted by the outskirts of Sahuayo de Morelos, a sight that induced unsavory choking sounds not unlike those of an emphysema victim asking the price of a coffin. I passed him the joint, which he waved away. It isn't the *chora*, Señor Esteban, it's the dust. I will die coughing without something to cool my throat, and he pulled to the curb and shut off the engine. The car noise had been squatting fatly atop loud music, possibly an unbottled rumor of Pancho Villa's victory march. It seemed to be coming through the wall beside us.

Thanks to the Virgin this excellent cantina was nearby, Guillermo said with a clear voice. The women here, they know me as a valued customer, and the beer is very cold. He banged open his door and rolled into the street.

We went inside and down some steps to a large courtyard, Guillermo leading the way to a table near the band. He grabbed my arm, nodding in the direction of the barmaids. Do you see the *repisas* on the one to the left?

I squinted through the howl of several trumpets and an auditory crisis of cymbals. *Ripisas?*

Guillermo's forward eye locked on me while the other scanned the room. Those two round things on her chest, he said slowly as if talking to someone retarded. He cupped his hands and held his arms straight out and parallel, rotating his wrists as if turning knobs. Then he pushed his face full onto mine exhaling the bruised history of fermentation, the surprised hiccups of agave worms in their death throes. Esteban, I often wonder how you've survived so many years being such a, how do you say in English, *zurramato*?

Dumbass.

Exactly. But we need beer. You've been very generous, and I'd buy the first glass except car repairs and funeral expenses have left me temporarily in debt. Later, my friend, the girls come here and sit looking for men such as us, men of culture and good breeding. Follow my lead, Esteban, and you won't have any problems. I'm irresistible to women. We'll need rooms, of course, but we can rent two rooms right here above the courtyard. You need to pay in advance.

Okay, I said. I'll pay for the rooms. Go rent them and get us the best price. I need one with a shower, or a shower nearby. You can buy your own women.

I understand, *señor*, if you can find the generosity to lend me some pesos to pay for such comfort.

Aren't you still in mourning?

For an ordinary man, yes, the mourning period would still be in effect. Never forget that I'm tough, Señor Esteban, capable of enduring incredible hardship, including the death of my beloved Teresa. This is because I'm descended directly from the Conquistadors. The men of my family suffer deeply but without showing emotion, just as our ancestors once did in Spain. Then it's our tradition to recover quickly and move forward.

I thought your wife's name was Juanita.

That's what I just said. Weren't you listening? How do you say in English, *no mames*?

You're shitting me. I think so anyway, roughly. . . .

Exactly, Señor Esteban. That's how I feel this very minute. See how quickly I pick up your language? *Poosy*!

I wondered if the Conquistadors wore piss-stained trousers like their descendent sitting beside me, whether they were mobile homes for crab lice and their shirtsleeves repositories for mummified food. Probably so. Guillermo disappeared to rent two rooms taking some of my money. I was certain to get screwed, especially leveled as I was by this buzz that sat astride a moralizing elevation much larger than worry. The whole idea of it put a kink in my neck. To eat excessively of the bean does that, I said, or maybe I just thought it.

Then he was back, a scratching presence abruptly inside my personal fog. Where had he gone? Why had he left? He stood there as before in a campesino's shirt and pants looking off-white and lumpy, like ice cream melting on distressed pavement, and he was yelling, *señoritas*, Guillermo is here! This gringo and I need beer!

The barmaids turned, then laughed and swayed toward us, hair shiny and black in the tilted sun.